creative
MACHINE EMBROIDERY
A PRACTICAL SOURCEBOOK

GAIL HARKER

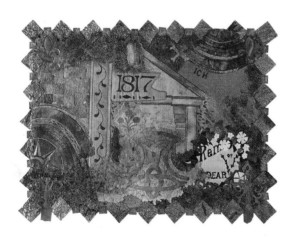

B.T.BATSFORD · LONDON

CONTENTS

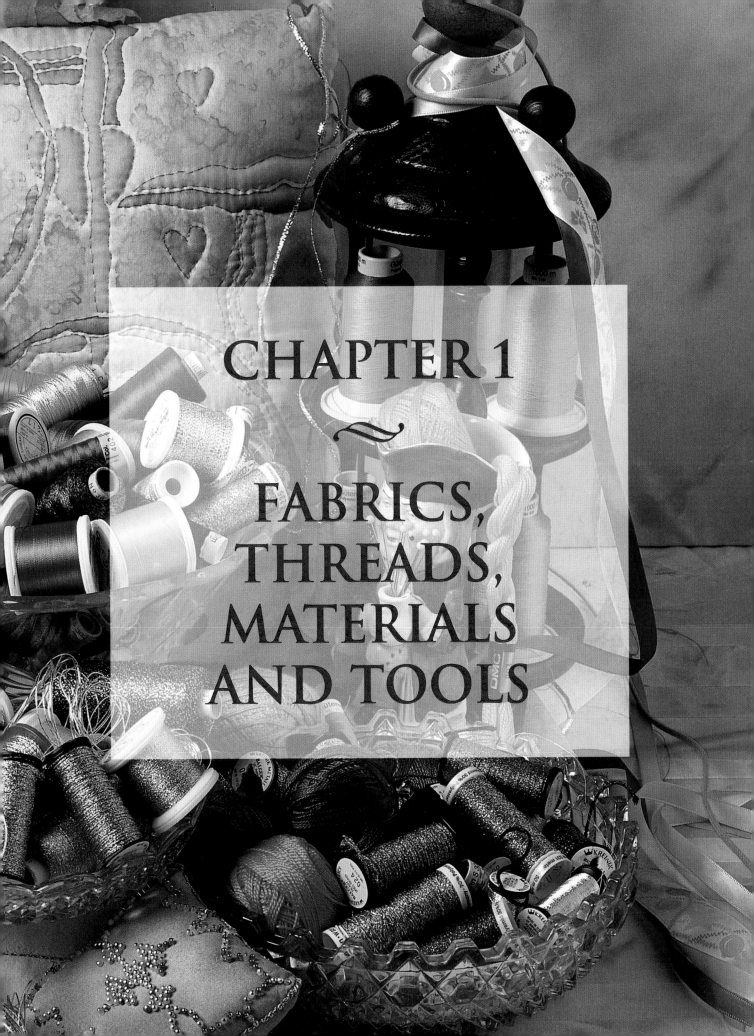

CHAPTER 1

~

FABRICS, THREADS, MATERIALS AND TOOLS

THE MACHINE

The most ordinary of electric zigzag sewing machines will be suitable for working the projects contained in this book, and nowadays almost any machine will provide you with additional stitches and patterns.

AUTOMATIC STITCHES

Automatic stitches have been developed by machine manufacturers to form an onboard library of utility or decorative stitches and are an evolutionary development of the original zigzag machines. These stitches are worked with the feed dogs engaged, and a foot attached to the presser bar.

MACHINE SET UP

Check your machine manual for instructions on changing tensions. Although some manuals may advise against this, it is essential to be able to adjust tensions on your machine. Certain machines have what is termed universal tension, and in theory these should not require adjustment. In practice, however, it is vital to be able to adjust tensions for specific machine embroidery techniques, and you will need to be prepared to readjust tensions a little as new stitch patterns, such as zigzag or other programmed patterns, are selected.

TOP (UPPER) TENSION

Top tension is adjustable by turning the indicated dial or knob. The scale usually ranges from 0 to 10: 0 represents no top tension; 3 to 5 is normal tension, and 6 to 10 will be very tight, or high tension. Some machines have no numerical scale at all, having instead a simple '+' or '-' indication on either side of a central or normal setting. It is worth noting that the perfect balance required for ordinary

◀◀ 1-1 A collection of machine embroidery threads, and hand embroidery threads - Perlé (Cotton Pearl), gold metallic. Pink silk fabric hand dyed by Graham Giles.

domestic sewing does not necessarily apply to machine embroidery; if only the upper side of the work will be seen, it is not important if the top thread shows slightly on the underside of the fabric.

REMOVABLE BOBBIN CASES

Wind the bobbin with the required thread and insert it into the bobbin case. Most bobbin cases have a set screw and a tension screw. The set screw holds the tension band in place. The tension screw is the one that may need adjustment. When adjusting the tension screw, only give the screw a half turn for each adjustment. Holding the bobbin case with the open side (the side where the bobbin is inserted) facing your body, turn the tension screw clockwise to increase tension or anticlockwise to reduce tension. Take care: this tiny screw has a tendency to pop out and is easily lost. Be sure to check your manual for specific instructions for your machine.

PURCHASING CHECK LIST

You can create free machine embroidery on almost any sewing machine, but the following are points to consider before you buy a new machine.

❋ Check whether the feed dogs can be lowered below the needle plate or not.

❋ If the feed dogs cannot be lowered, ensure that there is a cover plate that can be used to cover the feed dogs.

❋ A flat bed is preferable for machine embroidery. If the bed is sloping, ensure that an embroidery frame can be held tightly to the bed of the machine, with no gaps.

❋ Check that the bobbin case is easy to remove and reinsert into the machine.

THE FEED DOGS

When the feed dogs are up, as they are for most straightforward domestic sewing purposes, they move back and forth in a rolling up and down motion, feeding the fabric under the needle at a rate determined by the selected stitch pattern. Effectively, this action sets the length of each stitch. This is called automatic stitching, but in practice, straight stitch, zigzag, and other automatic decorative stitches can be used in a highly creative manner as the embroiderer alters the length and/or width of the stitches to form interesting patterns. Some machines are provided with scanning devices that allow patterns of this type to be stored in the computer memory for recall at will.

This description can only be a very general one, indicating the capabilities of any one of many machines, but each machine is different and the way to truly master the capabilities of your model is to study the manual for that model. You might even consider taking a basic course on machine operation from the vendor who sold you the machine.

For what is usually termed free machine embroidery, the feed dogs are lowered. This is accomplished in one of several ways, according to the machine. In some cases the feed dogs may be lowered by pressing a button, while other machines may a have a dial or disc to move them out of action. When the feed dogs are lowered and out of action, the fabric is no longer fed through the machine, leaving control of the length and width of each stitch in the hands of the embroiderer. Most manufacturers cover free machining in their manuals, though it may be described under a section entitled 'Darning' (both darning and free machining use the same basic technique).

FEET AND ATTACHMENTS

The feet and attachments named here are designed for specific types of programmed and free machine stitching. Check your machine manual to find which feet are available for your machine.

SATIN STITCH FOOT (EMBROIDERY FOOT)

The satin stitch presser foot has a groove on the underside of the foot to allow clearance of the high pile created by the stitches. This helps the fabric to feed through evenly.

DARNING FOOT

While most machines allow free machining without the use of a foot, the idiosyncrasies of individual machines (even among those produced by the same manufacturer) may demand the use of the darning foot. The darning foot assists in stabilizing fabric during free machine embroidery, and also acts as a safety guard to keep fingers from passing under the needle.

TEFLON FOOT (ROLLER FOOT)

This is designed to reduce friction while stitching on such fabrics as vinyl, plastics or leather.

OPEN TOE FOOT

This foot is sometimes called an embroidery foot, or appliqué foot. The toe of the foot is shorter than that of other feet, allowing the embroiderer to see the production of programmed stitches.

QUILTING FOOT

This is another of the specialized feet available for domestic sewing machines. Feet are available in a variety of sizes, some with an opening in the front.

MACHINE EMBROIDERY FRAMES

A frame will hold fabric tightly, enabling the user to control the material and providing a handhold with which to direct stitches while the feed dogs are lowered or disengaged and the presser foot removed. Allow an adequate overlap around the sides to ensure that the fabric is secure in the frame. Round embroidery frames or hoops come in a wide range of sizes and materials. Frames may be made of wood or a combination of plastic and metal. Wooden frames generally have a knurled screw on the outer ring to adjust for varying fabric thickness and tightness. Bind the inner ring of wood frames with narrow bias tape, stitching the end to secure it. The tape binding helps to reduce the likelihood of fabric slipping in the frame. Plastic frames are made with a groove on the inner face of the ring, which receives a springy inner ring made of metal. These frames are recommended for fine fabrics, such as silks and fine cotton. Rings larger than 12 cm (5″) may not adequately secure fabric for free machining, as it is important to ensure that the fabric held in the ring makes close contact with the needle plate, without gaps.

OTHER EQUIPMENT

SCISSORS
Use dressmakers' scissors for general fabric cutting and small sharp scissors for appliqué and other delicate cutting requirements.

TWEEZERS
These are handy for removing threads that may be wound around the bobbin case or caught in the feed dogs.

LINT BRUSH
Most machines are supplied with a brush to remove the lint that always seems to build up around the bobbin case and feed dogs.

SEWING MACHINE OIL
Most new generation machines are self-lubricating. Refer to your machine manual for oiling recommendations.

BOBBIN CASE
For convenience, keep two extra bobbin cases to hand, with one case set at the normal tension and the other at a much looser tension, for special effects.

BOBBINS
Be sure to have several bobbins wound with the appropriate threads for a quick change or to change colour.

NEEDLES

Needles react differently to thread types, fabric types and layers of fabric used. The wrong size needle that is burred or bent can often create stitch problems. Always work your own experiments to determine what is really best for your sampler.

Some needles have been developed to help solve special stitching problems. The following selection is of particular use to machine embroiderers.

Continental and US/English Needle Sizes									
Continental	60	65	70	75	80	90	100	110	120
US/English	8	9	10	11	12	14	16	18	20
		Very fine			Medium			Very heavy	

TOPSTITCH NEEDLE
This is an extra sharp needle with an eye that is about twice as long as the standard. It is the ideal choice for stitching with heavier thread, when two threads are threaded through the needle, or for stitching with metallic threads. Topstitch needles do not make large holes in the fabric, and are supplied in various sizes.

EMBROIDERY/METALLIC NEEDLE
Some stitching threads readily shred, break, or split as they suffer the rigours of passing through the eye of a needle and the fabric. The extra large eye of an embroidery needle gives additional space which reduces friction on the thread, while the grooved needle shaft helps to feed thread through the fabric, diminishing the risk of skipped stitches. (Note that free machine embroidery and quilting both put a lot of strain on a needle, so use good needles and change them often.)

SPRING NEEDLE
The spring needle was designed to be used in free machine embroidery and free machine quilting. The spring apparatus mounted on the needle shaft reduces the fabric bounce that may occur as the

needle is withdrawn from the fabric on the return passage, and may therefore eliminate the need for a darning foot. Do not throw this needle away if it breaks or gets dull. Instead, remove the spring apparatus; slide it over a new needle, and then dispose of the broken needle.

SELF-THREADING NEEDLE

The self-threading needle has a thin slot on the side through which the thread passes into the eye when it is drawn across. These needles are very helpful for those who have trouble threading needles, but they are not as durable as other types.

▲ 1-2 *The Cloutie Tree*
2.4 x 1.8 m (8 x 6 ft) - The artist was inspired by the practise in some societies of tying ribbons to a tree in order to commune with nature. Free machine embroidery was applied on calico (muslin).

Margaret Hall

Hem stitch/wing needle

This needle is manufactured with a wing or flange on each side of the shaft. It is effective in separating the fibres of some of the natural-fibre fabrics, such as cotton organdie. The needle produces a larger than usual entry hole, which can create an artistic effect when certain programmed decorative stitches are being used.

Jeans/denim needles

The jeans needle has been specifically produced for stitching on heavy fabrics and is excellent for machine embroidery on such fabrics.

Quilting needle

The quilting needle has a deep point that is thin and tapered, making it very useful when stitching multiple layers of fabric, as in machine quilting.

FABRICS FOR MACHINE EMBROIDERY

Over the years, fabrics have undergone a radical transformation. Sourcing unusual or inspiring fabrics can be a huge challenge. Different countries have access to many different types of fabrics. In addition to this, a fabric that is known by a trade or generic name in one country may be available in other areas of the world under a completely different name. To overcome some of the ensuing difficulties, it is important to gain a knowledge of the weight and feel of suitable fabrics, regardless of the name applied, bearing in mind that particular stitches and techniques tend to work best on certain types of fabric.

It is advisable to create a notebook of fabric samples. This should contain swatches of fabric, indicating when and where each was purchased and whether it is a regularly stocked item, its fibre content, the brand name, and any generic name used for that swatch. As work is done on one of these samples, record information about how it behaves with any particular stitch or technique, and how it reacts to manipulation, painting, or any other process used.

Almost any fabric may be used for machine embroidery. The main consideration is how well the fabric will support the weight of the thread and technique to be used. Many soft furnishing fabrics, sometimes known as upholstery fabrics, along with traditional cottons, linen, and some dressmaking fabrics are suitable, as are some wool and synthetic blends. Some of these will be found in ordinary fabric shops or stores, but others may only be found in speciality shops or departments, such as bridal suppliers, specialist embroidery suppliers, or in shops selling furnishing materials. One's developed sense of feel for the fabric will dictate how any of these may work for the technique to be used. If the specific fabric suggested for a particular project is unobtainable, try to find a close substitute with a similar weight and texture.

FABRIC WEAVES

Plain weave

Most fabrics are produced with a plain weave, also known as tabby. This means that the fabric is woven using a regular over and under of both the warp and weft threads. Typical plain woven fabrics include calico, muslin, and organdie/organza, all of which are suitable for machine embroidery.

Twill

There are numbers of different types of twill weave. In general, the fabric appears to have a diagonal weave, where the weaving threads pass over two or more threads before dipping under the crossing thread. Typical examples of this weave are denim, ticking, and certain of the thinner cotton fabrics, some of which are suitable for machine embroidery.

Satin weave

This is produced with many variations. Satin weaves are worked with each warp yarn crossing over four filling or weft yarns, then passing under five weft yarns. Silk satin, cotton satin, and most cotton drapery linings have a satin weave. The effect of the weave is to produce a fabric that is shiny and frays very readily. Satin-weave fabrics can be very difficult to machine embroider.

TRANSPARENT FABRICS

COTTON ORGANDIE

Cotton organdie is a plain-weave fabric that is sheer and lightweight. The best quality is almost transparent and treated with a permanently stiff finish. Look for Swiss organdie; lesser qualities will be more opaque and slightly heavier, and the stiff finish may wash out.

SILK ORGANZA

Silk organza is a plain-weave, lightweight, diaphanous, transparent fabric. Its shiny, crisp texture accepts dyes and paints, and it has a pleasant sewing quality. When applying automatic stitches, it is advisable to back this fabric with more of the same, or with a heavier fabric. Alternatively, a tear-away paper product may be used to support the fabric while stitching. For free machine stitching, the fabric may be mounted in a round frame. It is also useful for stiffening other fabrics, as a backing, when stitching without a frame. Silk organza is a good option to consider when layered fabrics are called for, as it is suitable for quilting and appliqué both as a top and/or a bottom fabric. Use it for garments or wall hangings. Its resistance to fraying makes it an excellent fabric for cut-back appliqué, while one or more layers of silk organza can create a see-through water-colour effect when the fabrics are hand painted.

SILK ORGANDIE

Silk organdie is a plain-weave fabric that is slightly stiffer and more opaque than silk organza. Its qualities are very similar to those of cotton organdie.

NYLON ORGANZA

Nylon organza may be found under any number of different trade names. It is an even-weave fabric with a stiff consistency and is manufactured in many colours. It is sometimes woven to include metal threads, or with a sparkling effect, and examples may be found in abundance at bridal or costume fabric stores and in other specialist fabric shops. Its transparent qualities may vary from very sheer to nearly opaque. When it is being embroidered with automatic stitches, it will probably require backing or layering. For free machine stitching, it should be mounted in a frame with one or two layers. Its non-fraying qualities make this a good fabric for appliqué or cut-back appliqué. Edges may be sealed without turning by carefully singeing them with a soldering iron. Interesting and irregular edges can result from this technique.

FINE-GAUGE NET

Fine-gauge net, or tulle, is a crisp fabric available in nylon, rayon, and sometimes silk or cotton. Nylon net does not dye nor accept painting. The fabric does not fray and is suitable for layering, appliqué, and cut-back appliqué. It may also be used for stitching automatic patterns, and it is very good for free machining,. if layered and mounted in a frame.

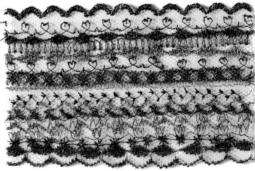

◄ 1-3 Nylon net provides a foundation for programmed decorative stitches creating a lace-like structure.

Penny Butterworth

▶ 1-4 Printed fabrics in various tones of beige take on much greater interest when rows of programmed stitches are applied. Stitches are shortened and lengthened at will while being stitched.
Penny Butterworth

OPAQUE FABRICS

COTTON CALICO/MUSLIN

Known as calico in Britain and muslin in America, this plain-weave fabric may either be soft or stiff and heavy. Unbleached types will have a matte, off-white or bone colour. The bleached fabric, however, will be white. During the manufacturing process, sizing is applied. This makes the fabric stiff, but it will probably be washed out if the calico/muslin is put through a hot wash. Automatic stitches work very well on this fabric, especially if it has been stiffened. It should be backed with iron-on interfacing or a tear-away paper product. Mounted in a round frame, it accepts free machine stitches very well. Some muslin is quite stretchy across the nap and may distort under stitching. Try putting two layers in the frame.

COTTON TWILL

Cotton twill comes in a range of weights and names. It is suitable for automatic stitching as well as for free machine embroidery. Look for the twill fabric that is lighter than either denim or ticking and is usually found in white. Either side of the fabric may be used, but the reverse side is smoother, more regular, and does not display the diagonal weave appearance of the right side. The fabric is good for creating programmed stitch samples and free machine samples with a build-up of massed stitches.

QUILTER'S COTTON

Quilter's cotton is not a label one would find on a bolt of fabric. For the purposes of this book, it is defined as any good quality dress-weight cotton fabric, and will be found at fabric shops in a variety of solid colours and prints. Cottons of this type are very suitable for both continuous line quilting and appliqué techniques. Dress-weight cottons, however, do not support a heavy build up of dense stitches.

FLANNELETTE

Flannelette is found in both plain and twill weaves. The fabric has a light, raised nap on one side and is often used for children's nightwear. Stitched with the nap upwards, it may be used as a backing for layered fabrics or for quilting.

EVEN-WEAVE FABRICS

HESSIAN/BURLAP

Hessian, burlap, and another similar fabric may be known as gunny, or coarse sacking material. These fabrics have a distinctive odour due to the jute or sisal fibres from which they are woven. The loose nature of the weave makes a fabric of this type an obvious candidate for drawn-thread work, while automatic decorative stitches worked over the fabric will create a lacy effect as strands of the fabric are pulled together, producing open areas.

PLASTERER'S SCRIM

Scrim is a term that is defined as a fabric with a plain, loose weave. A variant of this fabric, with a more open, loose weave than usual, was originally manufactured for professional plasterers, who embed it in

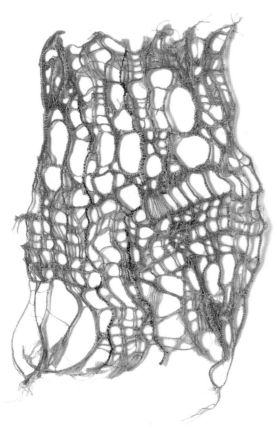

◄◄ 1-5 Free zigzag stitch worked on plasterer's scrim in a frame over vertical and horizontal threads.

◄ 1-6 Programmed stitches worked over linen scrim. Some fabric threads have been withdrawn to create a lacy effect.

Penny Butterworth

fragile plaster work to add reinforcement. This very loose type of scrim fabric is suitable for both free machine embroidery (the fabric must be held in a frame) and automatic stitching, and will create an open, lacy effect.

LINEN SCRIM

Linen scrim, by definition, is a fabric woven from flax fibres with an obvious plain weave. It is similar to the above, though not as coarse, and is heavier than gauze, but with a clearly defined weave. Linen scrim is suitable for automatic stitches, which create lacy structures on this ground, and for drawn-thread work.

LINEN

Other linen fabrics (more closely woven than scrim) can be very expensive and are prescribed for a wide range of both hand and machine embroidery techniques. The more usual linens will have a true even weave, and the available range extends from very

light to extremely heavy. They are obvious candidates for even-weave techniques worked through machine embroidery. Automatic stitches are very effective on linen, with the weave acting as a governing influence on the work. The fact that the fabric threads can be counted accurately makes even-weave linens an ideal choice for geometric patterns.

CHEESECLOTH

Cheesecloth is a soft loosely woven fabric that is supplied in various gauges (the gauge relates to the number of threads per 2.5 cm/1˝). Some gauges are very sheer, while those with a higher thread count will be more opaque. Many shops selling either kitchen supplies or fabric will stock cheesecloth. Regardless of the gauge selected, the fabric will open up, creating a lacy effect when stitched. Try mounting it in an embroidery frame. Cheesecloth also takes dyes very well. Butter muslin is a British variant which is so similar to ordinary cheesecloth that quite frankly there is no perceptible difference between the two.

▶ 1-7 Description of Borders -
Top to Bottom
Jagged Point Edges - A colour photocopy was first painted with water colour. Over this, fabric pieces were arranged. Silk organza was fused over the fabric and paper. Jagged, pointed edges were then cut using scissors. Straight stitch was worked over the top with the feed dogs up (engaged).

Satin Stitch Edge - Machine embroidery thread was arranged over cotton backing. Silk organza was fused over all. Straight and zigzag stitches were worked over the whole piece. The satin stitch edge was worked before the excess fabric was trimmed from the edges.

Acetate Fabric - Holes in the fabric and edges were burned using a soldering iron. No stitching was applied.

Silk Organza - Two layers of silk organza were fused together. Straight stitch was worked along the edge and excess fabric was then trimmed away.

A bottom layer of satin acetate has been sprinkled with beads, sequins, and threads. Over this a piece of nylon organza was laid, and fused to the bottom layer. Free running stitch was worked by machine. Buttonhole rings and buttonhole edging was worked by hand.

OTHER MACHINE EMBROIDERY FABRICS

Besides the fabrics already discussed and those mentioned below, there are many interesting fabrics that could be used in machine embroidery. Some might be used for small pieces of appliqué, while others might provide an interesting stitch background. It is for the embroiderer to experiment and come to her own conclusions about each fabric.

FELT

Felt is a non-woven fabric commercially available in a number of qualities and fibres. Some felts are made of wool and others of synthetic fibres. The thickness, flexibility, and sewing suitability of felts can vary tremendously. Hand-made felt is not discussed in any of the examples, but could be used if desired. Felt is excellent as a bottom fabric for sandwiched fabric layers used in free machine stitching

MELTON

Melton is a very firm wool fabric with a lightly felted nap. It is useful for doing free machine embroidery without a frame, and is also suitable for a bottom layer of fabric.

LAMÉ

Lamé is highly frayable, but the bonded variety has its uses for creating certain special effects in appliqué.

IMITATION SUEDE

Imitation suede is commonly available in America as Ultrasuede. This expensive fabric, which is available in weights ranging from very light to medium, looks like suede and may be used where a suede-like appearance is desired. As it not only looks but handles like suede, no edge treatment is necessary, which makes it ideal for appliqué.

SILKS

Silk fabrics, only some of which have already been mentioned, are a world unto themselves. The lustrous sheen of some silk fabrics contributes a beautiful finish to quilting. Silk patchwork can be a visual knockout. Some silk fabrics, however, are very stretchy, and these can be difficult materials upon which to work machine embroidery. In this case, backing is called for. Fraying is another factor that needs to be considered when using silks.

INTERFACINGS

FUSIBLE INTERFACINGS

Most shops supplying dressmakers will have interfacings in a wide range of weights. Iron-on interfacings are manufactured with a fusing agent applied to one side and are especially useful when fused to lightweight fabrics, making them more suitable for machine embroidery. Always follow the manufacturer's instructions when fusing an interfacing to fabric.

PLAIN INTERFACINGS

Other non-woven interfacings are supplied without any fusing agent. These are generally used as stiffening for other applications, such as the child's waistcoat on page 71.

PELMET VILENE

Pelmet vilene (British) was developed to provide stiffness for pelmets and curtain headings. An American alternative, known as Timtex, was developed as a stiffener for hat brims and belts. Machine embroiderers are quick to discover that products meant for other purposes can be useful for any number of embroidery applications. Both of these products may be painted, layered or fused. They will also accept dense machine stitching, and are suitable for both free and automatic techniques. Try using them for book covers, bags, wall hangings, and other sturdy, attractive, constructions.

FUSIBLE WEBBING

Fusible webbing is known by a number of different

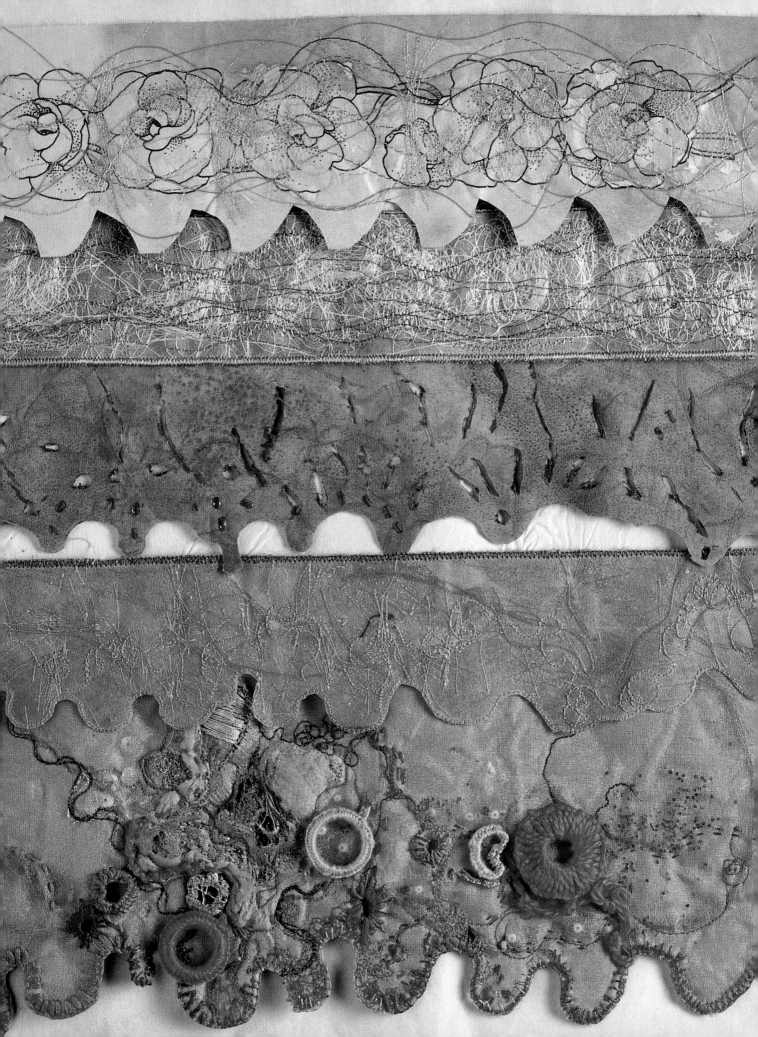

names, depending upon the manufacturer and where it is marketed. It is essentially a heat-sensitive fusing agent (double sided) applied to a paper backing and covered by a protective paper to allow bonding on one side at a time. The webbing is supplied in various weights and fusing strengths, and is useful for bonding one fabric to another to create fabric layers. Always follow the manufacturer's instructions. All fusible products may not react in the same way.

BATTING

Batting (also known as wadding) is supplied in a vast array of types, sizes and qualities. Batting is useful to the machine embroiderer as support for machine stitching on layered fabrics. The batting, while not needed for bulk, improves the ability to move fabric layers under the needle when stitching without a frame. For machine embroidery, find the thinnest, softest product available. The material could be manufactured from wool, cotton, silk, or synthetic fibres. The amount of loft that a type of batting may have is not always indicated. Some may be labelled low loft, or light batting. Use a ruler to measure the depth or thickness. Batting of 50 mm ($1/4"$) is considered thin. If the batting is thicker, it may sometimes be split into thinner layers. Also look for alternatives to batting; these may be made of natural or synthetic fibres.

DOMETTE

Domette is a soft open-weave fabric usually made either of wool or a wool blend. The material has a long nap, making it useful both as padding and as interlining for quilting.

DISAPPEARING FABRICS

These fabrics are used to make lace or new fabric. In most cases it is possible to draw a design on a disappearing fabric before stitching. The design will disappear with the fabric.

COLD-WATER-SOLUBLE FABRIC

This looks rather like plastic wrap and, as with other non-woven fabrics, is manufactured under various trade names. A ball-point machine needle is generally the choice for stitching into this fabric by machine. If you have problems with thread breakage, try other needle types. If a specific design is being created, it is important to ensure that the stitches are interlocked across the whole piece. The grid of interlocking stitches (geometric or not) will hold the design elements in position when the backing is dissolved. Do not stitch too densely in any area at one time as this will tend to break up the plastic; instead, when you are building up heavier areas, stitch a little at a time, returning from time to time to add more stitching. When all the stitching has been applied, the fabric is dipped into cold water, which causes it to dissolve, leaving behind the stitching. Rinse the stitching in running warm water to help remove the gummy residue.

HOT-WATER-SOLUBLE FABRIC

A fabric dissolved in hot water is also available. It works in the same way as cold-water solubles, but the hot-water method may cause some shrinkage of threads. Follow the manufacturer's instructions.

HEAT-DISSOLVING FABRIC

Other disappearing fabrics, variously known as vanishing muslin, heat away and similar names, provide a backing for machine embroidery before being removed by ironing. Pressing the work applied to this fabric must be done with a very hot iron with no ironing motion and no steam. Cover the stitched fabric with lightweight cloth or paper before pressing. Turn the front of the embroidery face down on the ironing board, away from the direct heat of the iron. Experiment on threads you wish to use before starting a project. Some threads may lose their lustre or deteriorate when they are heated. Use a good quality of machine embroidery thread for best effects. Move the iron from place to

◄ 1-8 Decorative stitches and lettering beautify otherwise plain ribbons. The ribbons are tacked (basted) to a much longer and wider piece of tear away stabiliser before stitches are applied. The ribbon edges may be singed to prevent fraying, or turned under.

Gillian Swift

place on both sides until the material has charred (it turns brownish black). Rub the fabric between the hands, as if washing it, to remove the blackened ash. More than one attempt at ironing out the soluble fabric may be necessary. Remaining ash may have to be gently removed with a toothbrush.

RIBBONS

Ribbons may be found in a profuse variety of textures, colours, designs, and widths, and can be divided into two main categories: craft ribbons, which are treated to stiffen them, in some cases having a wired edge, and woven-edge ribbons, which are narrow strips of washable fabric with selvages down each side. If you are making an item that will be washed, opt for the woven-edge type. Craft shops and florists will be good sources for craft ribbons. Woven-edge ribbons will most often be found in shops specializing in needlework or sewing notions.

The following woven-edge ribbons are particularly suited to appliqué.

Satin ribbons
These may be double faced (shiny on both sides) and are too heavy to be ideal for most projects. Single-faced satin ribbons are shiny on one side and matte on the other and are excellent for most machine embroidery projects.

Sheers
These fine, almost transparent ribbons are wonderful for overlaying and creating muted watercolour effects.

Metallics
These are made from or incorporate metallic or pearlized fibres.

THREADS FOR MACHINE EMBROIDERY

Almost every thread in the market place was developed for specific applications. Threads manufactured with a high degree of twist, making them strong and durable, are essential to the manufacture of clothing. The high twist prevents stitches formed with these threads from spreading, which would draw attention to their colour and lustre. Machine embroidery threads are not spun to such a high twist. This means that they are less strong, but they spread beautifully on fabric as they are applied, revealing their lovely colour and sheen.

Machine embroidery threads are supplied by a number of manufacturers and in a wide range of fibres, including cotton, silk, rayon, polyester, metallics, or blends of several fibres. The threads are available in different sizes, ranging from No. 100 (very thin) to No. 10 (thick), but the usual size range is between 30 and 40. Some threads are unnumbered or have no size designation.

A slight reduction of the top tension on your machine might make stitching with machine embroidery threads easier. The colour of the bobbin thread is not extremely important for machine embroidery so long as the back of the fabric will not be seen. If the back is to be seen, you must take the colour and type of bobbin thread into account to produce an attractive finish. Always test threads for suitability before using them for a project. The test will determine whether your machine is able to handle the thread and stitches.

It is a good idea to keep a notebook containing small samples with notations alongside. All machines have their own idiosyncrasies with regard to how they handle different threads. Keep records of machine settings and reactions to various threads to guarantee that you will be able to produce a desired effect. It is impossible to discuss threads without looking at other factors that cause threads to react in certain ways. Keep a simple chart alongside the threads in your note book, listing relevant information as shown below.

Top tension	Framed or not	Needle type and size
Bobbin thread	Free machinery (feed dogs down)	Foot type
Bobbin tension	Stitch type	Fabric type
	Automatic (feed dogs up)	

If a thread breaks, determine where it breaks. Variations in any of the above could produce entirely different effects. It is possible to use different types of threads on top and bobbin, but only if you are prepared to work through a period of trial and error adjustments on your machine.

BOBBIN THREADS

The bobbin tension is pre-set at the factory for ordinary domestic sewing purposes, using threads of high twist and density compared with machine embroidery threads. In most cases you will need to alter the bobbin tension if you are using anything other than dressmakers' thread. Listed below are a few general ideas about finding the correct tension when making decorative stitches on the top of the fabric using either automatic (feed dogs up) or free (feed dogs down) machine embroidery.

Different threads may be used in the bobbin, depending upon the particular machine used and effect sought after. Ordinary No. 30 or 50 cotton machine embroidery thread – the same thread as might be used on the top of the machine – works well in the bobbin of some machines. These fine threads will usually require an increase of bobbin tension if the thread is not to show on the top of the fabric.

SPECIAL BOBBIN THREADS
Special bobbin threads are available either in large spools or as pop-in bobbins. The composition of such threads varies, but they are generally available in very thin weights, up to No. 100, and in black or white. A thread of this type creates less thread build-up on the underside of the fabric, but you will need to increase the bobbin tension by tightening the screw on the bobbin case. Unless one is stitching with the same thread on the top of the machine (which is not normally the case), there will be a radical difference in thread weight between top and bobbin. Some machines do not take well to a major difference in thread weight.

RAYON OR SILKY-TYPE THREADS
These may or may not (depending on the machine) display the effect of looser bobbin tension, which may cause more of the bobbin thread to be brought up to the surface of the fabric. This is good only if you are planning this effect.

DRESSMAKERS' THREADS
If a shop selling machine embroidery thread is not very handy, ordinary dressmakers' thread may be used in the bobbin and will work fairly well on heavier fabric. Watch for a very heavy thread build up on the underside of the fabric. This type of thread may have a tendency to pucker the fabric unless it is framed. If you are using dressmakers' thread in the bobbin with Nos 30, 40 or 50 machine embroidery thread on top, the bobbin thread may pull the top thread to the underside of the fabric. If this occurs, loosen the bobbin tension or increase the top tension.

HAND EMBROIDERY THREADS

Many of the threads used in hand embroidery can also be used for machine stitching. These are manufactured from a wide range of fibres: cotton, silk, wool, linen, synthetics (such as rayon and polyester) and metal. Cotton, wool, and polyester threads are the most readily available, and are made in the widest variety of colours.

COTON À BRODER

Also known as Brilliant Cut Work and Embroidery thread, this has a very light twist, and is a soft looking, single cotton thread with a somewhat shiny surface, used for hand stitching.

COTTON PERLÉ

Pearl cotton is a mercerized cotton thread with a very shiny finish. It is supplied in skeins or balls, and has a more pronounced twist than six-stranded cotton, but it cannot be split. It produces an embossed effect when stitched. Sizes range from 16, 12, 8 and 5, to 3. Sizes 8 and 5 work as well for cable stitch by machine as for hand stitching.

CREWEL WOOL

For machine purposes, this is most often used for couching.

KNITTING, WEAVING AND CROCHET YARNS

These come in a wide range of fibres, thicknesses and colours. As well as the main purposes for which they are produced, they can be used for machine couching.

SILK THREAD

Silk threads have a high sheen and may be either stranded or twisted.

SIX-STRANDED COTTON

Also known as stranded floss, this lustrous, mercerized, pure cotton thread is available in about four hundred colours. It consists of lightly twisted strands which are supplied in skeins. Although designed for hand embroidery, these threads may be wound on the bobbin for cable stitch or for couching by machine.

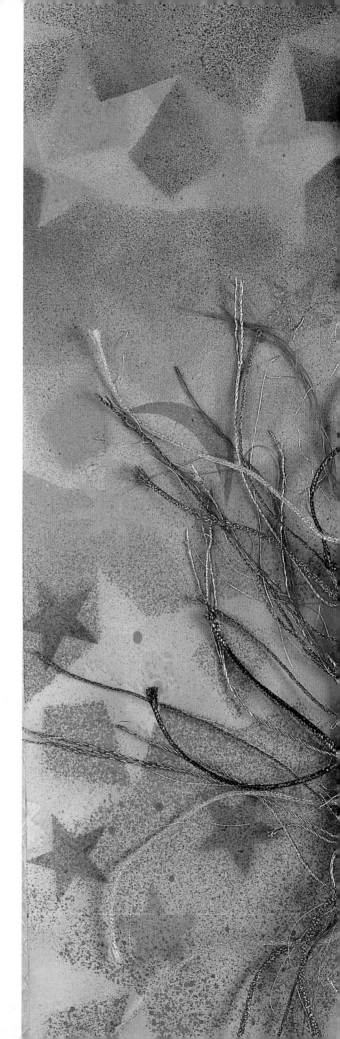

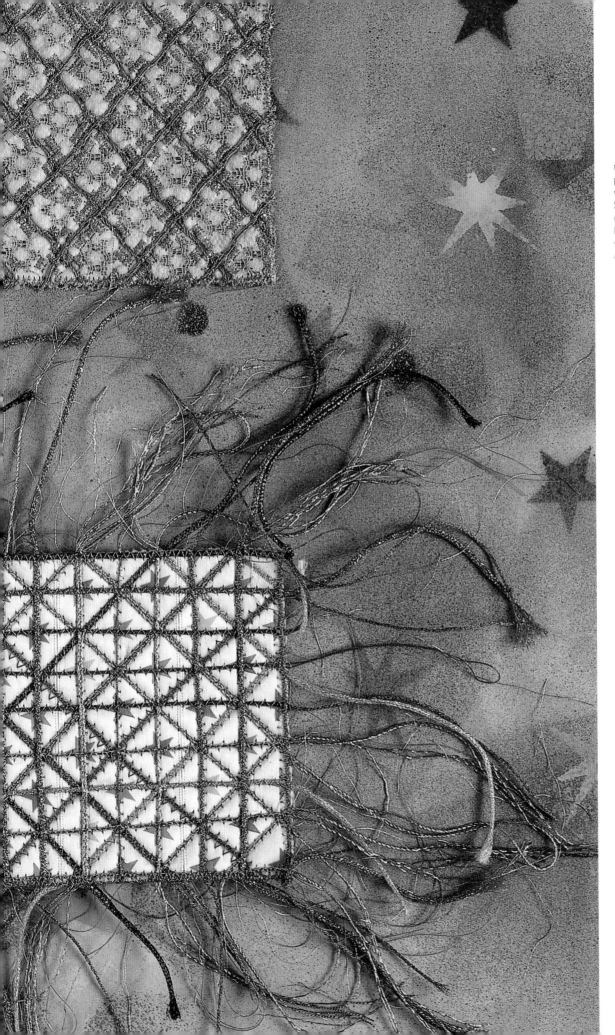

1-9 Couched Threads - Metal threads are arranged in a grid pattern and attached using a stitch wide enough to encompass them. Stitched with feed dogs up (engaged). One sample was prepared by fusing net and ribbon to pelmet vilene (Timtex) before stitching the decorative fringe.

CHAPTER 2

∼

INSPIRATION
FOR IMAGE
AND THEME

STARTING AT THE BEGINNING

WHERE TO START? This is the age-old question for all artists. Nothing is more daunting to the painter than the sight of an empty canvas. For the writer, the blank sheet of paper is sometimes an overwhelming obstacle. For the embroiderer, the obstacle will be a piece of fabric, a handful of thread, and a needle. Where does the first stitch go, and which stitch will it be?

There are no simple answers to the question of finding that wonderful, creative theme or design. There are, however, some time-proven approaches to developing these themes and designs.

If we start at ground zero, how do we take the first steps? If there is no water in the swimming pool, it is very difficult to learn to swim. So it is with visual stimulation. As with the water in the pool, we must begin to immerse ourselves in the art we like. It does not matter what kind of art it is – just start collecting. Collect pictures cut from magazines, pictures from art books, prints of paintings at the art gallery, picture postcards, and your own photographs of objects you like. Make some very simple sketches of some of those things. Try looking at fruits and vegetables, whole or dissected. Many an artist has found inspiration in just such normally mundane objects. Look at flowers, insects, animals, birds, fish – and on we could go. All artists must surround themselves with articles of potential inspiration.

▲ 2-2 Flower inspiration from Denise Harrison's sampler.

▲ 2-3 Inspired from a floral design worked on a 19th century pincushion.

▼ 2-5 Border design from prehistoric art of the Southern Appalachian Indians. A human head or mask entwined with a stylised rattlesnake form was engraved on a piece of pottery. This is a fine example of an exciting design idea based upon dividing shapes with contrasting-line borders.

◄◄ 2-1 *The Fragment Series* 30 x 30 cm (12 x 12") This composition is made up of smaller separate samples called: The Fragment, Roundel, Elizabethan Fragment and The Long Band Sampler. Patterns in repeating borders and flowers in circles make up the structures. The artist's samplers were inspired from historic pictures from the Elizabethan period. The work has been produced by fusing paper and fabric and then by applying free machine stitches.
Denise Harrison

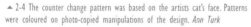

▲ 2-4 The counter change pattern was based on the artists cat's face. Patterns were coloured on photo-copied manipulations of the design. *Ann Turk*

▶ 2-6 Rectangles are divided into shapes of different widths. The contrast in widths will contribute to a more interesting composition.

ESTABLISH A STRUCTURE

An interesting sampler can often depend upon the structure one builds into it in advance of any needlework. Any square, rectangle or triangle can be divided into strips of different widths, or borders. These can offer the contrast that is needed for the shape. Using graph paper and pencil, try this exercise. Before thinking about stitching, see if you can make the structure more interesting.

Novice embroiderers, who are practising stitches, should draw the shapes and divisions to the same size as in the intended sampler. A good size for this exercise is about 7.5 × 10 cm (3 × 4″). Try practising different patterns using a pen or pencil. Draw without lifting the pen or pencil from the paper. This will help you to start thinking in terms of pattern. Quickly move on to prepare your sampler, and begin stitching within the inscribed borders.

◀ 2-7 Many different patterns have been created to fit the divided rectangle. Many of them relate directly to free machine embroidery.

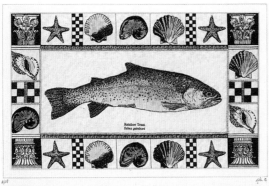

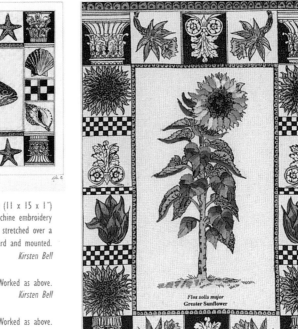

▲ 2-9 Rainbow Trout 28 x 38 x 2.5 cm (11 x 15 x 1″)
Screen printing and hand painting on calico (muslin). Free machine embroidery was added with the work in a round frame. The piece is stretched over a card and mounted.
Kirsten Bell

▶▲ 2-10 Sunflower 28 x 38 x 2.5 cm (11 x 15 x 1″) Worked as above.
Kirsten Bell

▼ 2-11 Grapes 28 x 38 x 2.5 cm (11 x 15 x 1″) Worked as above.
Kirsten Bell

▶▼ 2-12 Cauliflower 28 x 38 x 2.5 cm (11 x 15 x 1″) Worked as above.
Kirsten Bell

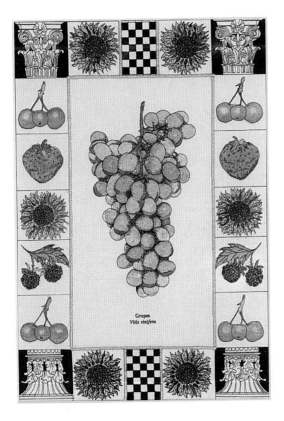

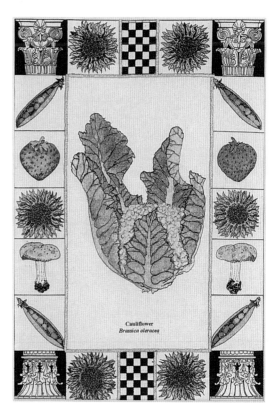

GRIDS

A grid may be constructed in a variety of ways. A repeating grid border may have different motifs within each shape. These will surround the central, more important, motif. When forged together, the elements will create a pleasing composition.

FIND AN INTERESTING MOTIF

There are many ways to develop a very simple motif into a more interesting form. Museums, copyright-free books and your own photos may suggest starting points.

Use tracing paper or vellum to trace a simple outline. You may need either to reduce or enlarge the outline to make work easier. Avoid all detail at this stage. Divide your chosen shape into more manageable divisions of space. Do not stop at one shape. Select and trace a few more to find the most pleasing design. Draw in lines (detail) to represent needle marks, or better yet, take a section of your drawing and trace it to the fabric to try out stitch patterns within the spaces. Try either programmed patterns (perhaps a zigzag) or free machine embroidery. When you have found the stitch effect that seems most suitable, embroider the whole piece of fabric, whether it is a sample or a finished work.

▲ 2-8 Grids can form some very interesting spaces in which to draw patterns. Grids may be totally geometric or irregular and curving. This exercise was first worked on graph paper by drawing different sized circles in each rectangle. A series of irregularly spaced lines form rays from the sun symbols. There are many variations one could play with in this exercise to create a lively pattern. See the Continuous Stitch Sampler (page 88) for another approach to this idea.

▲ 2-13 The eagle was inspired by a Byzantine decoration from the 12th Century. The shape has some very interesting edges. Half of this very interesting shape was drawn on graph paper, photocopied, and then copied to the opposite side, while checking to make sure the matching lines were in alignment.

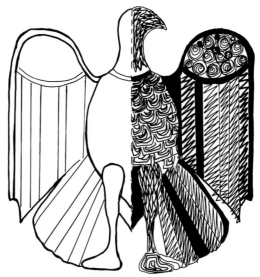

▲ 2-14 Half of the eagle has been divided into differently sized shapes. The other half of the design was filled in with stitch ideas.

▶ 2-15 The eagle's wing shows yet another pattern potential with feathery tassels hanging off the edge.

Experiment to find the surround or background shape that best suits the motif. Make some paper cut-outs to find which positive (the motif) and which negative (the background) shapes look most interesting together. To create really interesting shapes, make sure that the motif does not appear to float in too spacious a background.

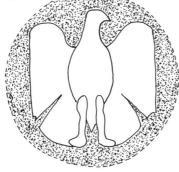

▲ 2-16 Draw a circle around the eagle shape to see how two shapes can fit together. The eagle forms the positive shape while the surrounding area is the negative.

▲ 2-17 The eagle enclosed within a square creates some interesting positive and negative effects provided by the contrast of the bird and the square. Cut a black paper square and lay a cut-out of the motif over it.

▲ 2-18 Placing the eagle within two squares surrounded by vermicelli patterning offers a more elaborate framing device for a simple subject.

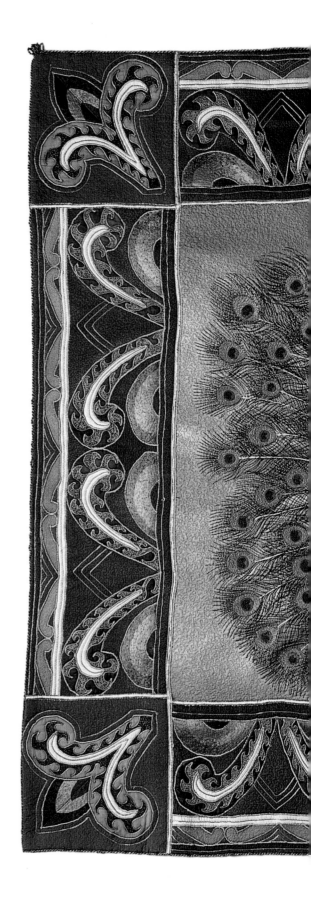

◄ 2-19 Peacock
69 x 92 cm (27 x 36″) Inspired
from a photograph, the artist first
drew a cartoon of the peacock on
paper using permanent ink pen.
The basic outline was traced to silk
fabric. The outlines on silk were
then painted with resist and left to
dry. When dry, areas of the design
were painted in with colour. The silk
was backed with wool felt. The piece
was mounted in a round frame to
do stitching and ironed each time
the frame was moved. The neck,
head and side feathers were worked
in free satin stitch, free running
stitch. Running stitch was also used
as a filling stitch.

Juanita Buchan

◄◄ 2-20 Detail of head and body.

◄ 2-21 Detail of border pattern.

PHOTOGRAPHS

Photographs, old or new, can prove a marvellous source of good ideas. Find a photograph that you would love to translate into an embroidery. Within the photo, locate the shape or shapes you wish to incorporate. If this process is new to you, try to find a photo that is not too cluttered with extraneous or distracting elements.

Lay a piece of vellum or tracing paper over the photo and trace around the shape. If the shape is too small to allow a good tracing, make an enlarged photocopy of a suitable size. After tracing, simplify the drawing. Eliminate all but the essential details and rearrange the picture, if necessary, to achieve a pleasing appearance.

▲ 2-23 Seagull Sample 12.5 x 18 cm (5 x 7″) The artist developed her theme by carving a rubber printing block with a lino carving tool. The resulting stamp was used to print repeating and random bird shapes on paper and hand painted fabric.   *Penny Butterworth*

▶ 2-24 Seascape 61 x 74 cm (24 x 29″) The motifs for this piece of patchwork were symbols of the sea: lighthouse, sailboats, barges and seagulls. The motifs were randomly arranged on the background fabric that was marbled to represent the feeling of the seaside.   *Penny Butterworth*

◀ 2-25 Photo
Close up of patchwork showing the boat designs that were scanned into the artist's computerised sewing machine and stitched on stabilized fabric. The gulls and lighthouse motifs were imprinted using the rubber stamp method with fabric paint..

▶ 2-26 Drawing from a Sketchbook - Boy and Dog
The original drawing was 14 cm (5½") high. I like to draw in the same size I imagine the work will be. Once I had started sampling stitch and technique ideas, I thought I might have to make the drawing a little larger. It is almost impossible to settle on the finished size until some areas have had some stitches worked.

▶▶ 2-27 Drawing from a Sketchbook - Boy and Dog
First Ideas for Stitches - Small pieces of organza were laid in overlapping fashion on the background fabric to try to create radiant light and aura. Free running stitch is applied causing a mixing of the fabric colours to create a feeling of energy. Free zigzag stitches were worked in the bottom portion. I would then select one of these techniques for use in my proposed new work.

▶▶ 2-28 Courtesy of New Harmony Gallery of Contemporary Art
In Praise of Old Women 76 cm x 81 cm (30 x 32") A quilt depicting a woman peering out from the centre of log cabin patchwork. Flowers cut from a floral print are appliquéd (Broderie Perse) around the motif. Other motifs were applied over the whole piece with rubber stamps.   *Sharon Doyle*

WORKING WITH THE IMAGE

The example I have chosen came from a family photo that included not only the boy and dog, but his brother and grandmother. I eliminated two of those figures and moved the window to a more pleasing position. The house and dog were significant to the boy. The dog was his best pal, and the house was one his mother and friends had built during the very hard times of the Great Depression.

After closely scrutinizing the darkened old photo, I decided not to attempt a fully representational reproduction, aiming instead for a likeness of the boy and dog. I used the surrounding shadows to place them in a world of ethereal light, innocence, and happiness.

STITCHING

I tried some sample stitching for each of the main areas of the composition. For your own creation on a similar photographic theme, start with some ideas for representing the texture on the side of the house.

Look for a combination of colour and effects that will portray your intention. Coloured pencils may help to give a quick and usable way of presenting the subject matter. Try some machine stitching ideas for the human subject on layered fabric. The aura of the surrounding background and shadow could be a collage built up of transparent fabric over the example intended for the house texture. The physical sampling of stitch and technique ideas is always more effective than trying to imagine effects.

SAMPLE GUIDELINES

Outline the ideas you would like to test.

Be prepared to change from the initial vision if the samples so indicate.

Work within your own skill level – this could mean simplifying the way in which you choose to develop your picture in stitches.

Expect the unexpected.

Try to put the ideas from the best of the samples into the finished piece.

WHY DOESN'T SOMEBODY WAKE UP TO THE BEAUTY OF OLD WOMEN?

SO MUCH HAS BEEN SAID AND SUNG OF BEAUTIFUL YOUNG GIRLS,

HARRIET BEECHER STOWE – 1852

CHAPTER 3

~

PREPARE
TO STITCH

PREPARE A SAMPLER

BEFORE ANY OTHER PREPARATIONS, measure your selected fabric and estimate how much of the total area will contain stitching (this will be the finished size). Make sure that the fabric is sufficiently large to allow a margin allowance of from 2.5 to 5 cm (1 to 2″) along all sides. The margin allowance assists in various ways, as listed below.

 It allows space for a frame with which to keep the fabric taut without encroaching upon the stitching area.

 It offers a start-up space for programmed stitches, avoiding the need for backstitching to secure the thread (see page 70).

 If you are free machining without a frame, the allowance will provide a secure hand hold around the edges of the fabric, permitting the necessary pushing and pulling actions as the fabric is moved across the needle plate.

MARKING THE SAMPLER

Step 1

Remembering to add margin allowances, measure the outside edges accurately, using a right angle and ruler, and trim away excess fabric. This is so that all corners will be squared and you will begin with a perfect rectangle or square.

3-1 *Dancing Roosters* 45 x 70 cm (18 x 28″) Wall hanging. Ivanovna Bystrove, by permission Shirley Berlin Private Collection

▶ 3-5 Step 1
(Marking the sampler)

▶▶ 3-6 Step 2

▼▶ 3-7 Step 3

▼▶▶ 3-8 Step 4

Step 2

Mark the inner line between the margin and the embroidery area on the fabric. This is easily accomplished by tracing around the inside of a shape cut to the correct size from a matt board. Use a light pencil or dressmakers' pencil.

Step 3

Alternatively, accurately cut a card of the correct size.

Lay this over the planned stitching area and lightly mark around the outside edges.

Step 4

Use running stitch to stitch along the lines marked out in step 2 or 3, delineating the proposed stitch area. This ensures that the edges of the work will be seen even if the pencil marks rub off.

HAND BASTING

Machine embroidery is frequently worked on layered fabric – a top layer, a middle layer of batting and, perhaps, a bottom layer. There are several reasons for this: the layers may enable you to use free machining techniques without a frame (see page 76); quilting techniques can be combined with other stitchery; the loft created by the layers adds further interest to the texture of your work, and delicate top fabrics, which would not otherwise readily support intensive machine stitchery, can be embroidered.

I have often been accused of treating the need to tack or baste the fabric layers by hand as some sort of religious experience. This step is often seen as labori-

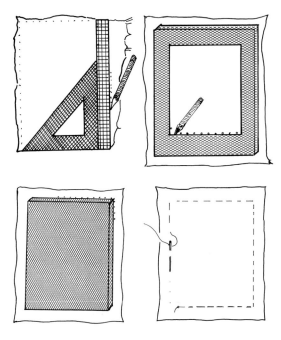

ous and unnecessary, but fabrics that have not been properly basted can pucker or distort in unwanted ways. I have seen in my own work, and that of many students, that skipping this step can result in having to begin all over again after getting half to three-quarters of the way through a project.

There are several advantages to basting by hand as opposed to machine stitching.

 It is possible to smooth out all the layers of fabric on a flat surface.

 It is easier to distribute wrinkles or other irregularities in the fabrics evenly.

 There is less distortion and stretching of fabrics while they are being basted together.

Baste layers of fabric on a table or other flat surface (not on the lap). Use a fine quilting needle with machine embroidery thread, and take stitches no longer than 1.5 cm (¾˝). The purpose is to have all the fabrics in the basted layers react as one, rather than shifting apart. Basting lines should be approximately 5 cm (2˝) apart. While it is possible to pin very small samples together, it will soon become apparent that layers will distort under most embroidery techniques.

PREPARE AND BASTE A SAMPLER

Step 1
Stitch from corner to corner on layered fabrics, creating an 'X' across the whole piece.

Step 2
Stitch a horizontal and vertical line through the centre of the 'X', creating a '+' across the fabric.

Step 3
Stitch a square around the centre of the fabric where the crosses meet.

Step 4
Continue stitching concentric squares, moving outward from the centre. This will result in many compartments across the whole fabric.

PREPARE AND BASTE LARGE ITEMS

Step 1
Assemble the layers on a flat surface and begin to baste them together, using running stitch. Work a vertical line and then a horizontal crossing line through the centre of the fabric. Begin at an edge and work across to the opposite edge.

Step 2
Alternately stitch horizontal and vertical rows about 5 cm (2˝) apart from the initial centre rows. Change stitch directions with each row (for example, stitching from top to bottom and then from bottom to top).

Step 3
Continue basting rows as above until the fabric is completely tacked.

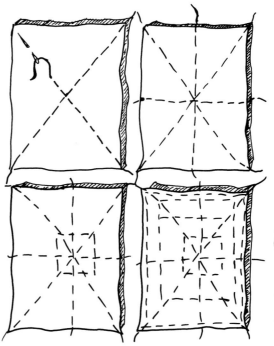

◀◀ 3-9 Step 1
(Prepare to tack fabric layers)

◀ 3-10 Step 2

▼◀◀ 3-11 Step 3

▼◀ 3-12 Step 4

▶ 3-13 Step 1
(Prepare and tack for larger items)

▶▶ 3-14 Step 2

▼▶ 3-15 Step 3

▼▶▶ 3-16 Step 4

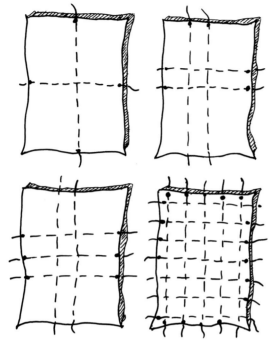

Step 4

The last rows of stitches will be on the outside edges of the fabric.

TRANSFERRING A DESIGN TO FABRIC

When your design is completed, you will need to transfer it to the fabric. Several products, some of which are listed below, are available for this purpose. Be sure to test any of these on a sample of your fabric before you commit yourself to using it for a special project.

AIR-SOLUBLE FELT-TIP MARKER

This type of marker makes a line – generally blue or purple – that fades from sight after about 24 hours. Markers vary in performance, depending on the manufacturer and the type of fabric used, so always make a trial sample before marking the main piece of fabric. Use a very light touch and mark as small an area of the design as possible.

TAILOR'S/DRESSMAKER'S CHALK

These chalks are often made in the form of a normal writing pencil, or as a wedge of chalk-like material with thin edges. They are generally an off-white or yellow colour, and are therefore more visible when used on darker fabrics. The chalk can be brushed off the fabric once the design has been stitched (the pencil variety often comes with a small brush at the top end for this purpose).

WATER-SOLUBLE FELT-TIP MARKER

This type of marker can be used to draw a design directly on to fabric, which is then erased after stitching. Some types of marker have one end as the drawing point, and the other end as the eraser. If yours only has the marking tip, use a cotton swab, moistened with water, to remove the lines. Always test this type of marker on a spare piece of fabric before use.

PAINTING FABRIC

Before any stitching begins, painting and colour printing may be applied to your fabric to produce vivid creative effects that make wonderfully patterned backgrounds for embroidery. Different techniques are required for each colouring medium. Before using any of them, you must first wash the fabric in a mild detergent to remove all sizing and finishing materials that could interfere with the fabric's ability to accept the paint or dye. Allow the fabric to dry, then press to remove any creases.

MULTIPURPOSE FABRIC PAINTS

Many dyes are compounded in an emulsion base. Often called fabric paints, their creamy consistency makes them easy to use, and the colours may be heat-set (with an iron) for washability once the fabric has dried. Good makes of water-soluble fabric paint include Jacquard Textile Color, Dylon Colour Fun, and Deka (all available from craft suppliers, see page 127). These paints work particularly well on interfacing, though they can be used to colour many other types of fabric. The instructions on heat-setting the paints may vary slightly between different brands, so read the information on the package.

◄ 3-2 Grand Canyon Bag. 15 cm x 23 cm (6 x 9"). Photo by Gail Harker.

The design inspiration came from City and Guilds Part 1 Geological Design theme — the Grand Canyon. Fabric paints were used to colour the silk fabrics. Silk organza was burnt, layered and applied to a silk background, A Kumihimo cord was made and beaded fringe added to the edges.   *Penny Peters*

SILK PAINTS

Silk paints are too thin for printing on to fabric, but can be used to create a variety of stunning painted effects, such as all-over, even colourings to interesting mottled or spattered textures. Most natural and some synthetic fabrics may be coloured with silk paints.

USING SILK PAINTS

The chief requirement is a clear expanse of table, work surface or floor on which to work and then leave the fabric to dry. You will also need jars of clean water, a paintbrush or small pieces of sponge and, of course, the paints in colours of your choice.

Lay down a large piece of plastic sheeting or other non-absorbent water-proof protective cover on the surface. This will not only protect the surface, but will also be instrumental in achieving certain mottled effects. Lay the fabric on the prepared surface. Spray or dip heavy fabrics or interfacing in water before applying colour, then squeeze them out and lay on the surface.

Prepare the paints by mixing them with a little water, referring to the manufacturer's instructions. The paints should have a fairly watery consistency, but be aware that the more water you add, the paler the colours will be. Brush or sponge the colours on the fabric, rinsing the brush before dipping into a new colour. Avoid over-saturation of very thin fabrics.

Leave the fabric to dry undisturbed overnight (silks and other light fabrics may dry in a few hours). A hairdryer may be used to accelerate the drying time, but this can have a tendency to halt the attractive mottled effects created when the fabric is left to dry naturally. If you do use a hairdryer, avoid spot-heating of sensitive fabrics such as silk.

When the fabric is completely dry, set or fix the paints, always referring to the manufacturer's instructions. Most silk paints may be set using an iron. Be sure to lay a pressing cloth over delicate fabrics. After setting, most fabrics will be colourfast in washing conditions usual for the fabric.

TRANSFERRING DESIGNS TO THE BACK OF A FABRIC

This technique for applying a design to the wrong side of the fabric is especially useful for appliqué. Start by basting together two fabrics of the same size: one will serve as the background fabric, while the other will become the appliqué fabric.

Draw the design on a sheet of tracing paper. Turn the paper over (right side down) and pin it to the background fabric. This is done to ensure that the image will not be seen in reverse on the right side of the fabric. Stitch along the design with automatic straight stitch, piercing the paper and fabrics. This will transfer the design to the fabrics. After you have stitched all the design lines, tear away the paper.

Turn the fabrics over so that the appliqué fabric is uppermost and cut away any excess fabric around the design. Finish the appliqué from the front (right) side, using free machine or automatic stitches.

BACKLIT DESIGN TRANSFER

Draw the design on lightweight paper, using a very dark felt-tip pen or pencil so that the design lines will be sufficiently clear to be seen through your fabric. Position the fabric over the paper and shine light through both. The design will be clearly visible through the fabric, allowing it to be traced with a tailor's marking pencil or a very hard drawing pencil.

If you do not have a light box, a window may provide a convenient light source. Simply tape the design to the window; position the fabric over the design, and tape it in place. If the transfer lines are likely to show through the finished stitching, you can reduce the amount of visible pencil by drawing dotted rather than solid lines.

TRANSFERRING CABLE STITCH DESIGNS

Since cable stitch is worked with the wrong side of the fabric uppermost, a cable stitch design may be drawn on the wrong side of the fabric. Unless the fabric is transparent, the design will be easy to follow and none of the design lines will show. Make sure when transferring the design that it will not be seen in reverse on the right side.

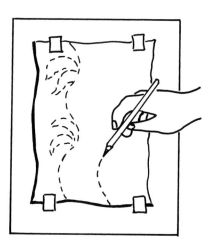

◀ 3-9 Transfer design to sheer fabric (such as silk organza) by placing the fabric over the paper design and tracing it using a dressmaker's (or 2H) pencil. Lightly trace the design.

▼ 3-4 *Nevern* 62.5 x 47.5 cm (25 x 19") Machine embroidery and appliqué on hand made paper.
Denise Harrison

CHAPTER 4

~

STITCHES AND TECHNIQUES

▶ 4-1 Photo - Mike Brown

13 Meerkats, 1 Aardvark and a Monkey - A waistcoat (vest) whose inspiration came from the artist's love for meerkats. Leather, cotton and dyed silk fabrics, along with mud cloth (woven and dyed in Mali, Central Africa) were used for the waistcoat. The colour is very dark brown and appears almost black. The animal shapes are appliquéd to vest using satin stitch and an overstitch (a programmed heirloom appliqué stitch on the artists machine). In addition to the animal shapes, she applied buttons, beads, rope, and threads pulled from African-made fabrics. Decorative metallic threads were used to work free satin stitch over the piece. The garment is lined with cotton fabric. *Virginia Schlosser*

◄ 4-2 Photo - Mike Brown
*13 Meerkats, 1 Aardvark and a
Monkey - A waistcoat - back.*

DECORATIVE STITCHES IN AUTOMATIC MODE

IT IS NOT ALWAYS EASY to impose one's will over automatic stitch patterns, as the stitches are programmed to produce their output in a predetermined way. However, straight lines and gentle curves of pattern are possible, and many pattern variations may be developed by changing the length and width of automatic stitches, and by using more than one thread through the top of the machine. In addition, it is interesting to experiment with one of more of the following techniques to alter the appearance of automatic patterns.

▼ 4-3 *Automatic Stitching on Paper* - Simple decorative stitches are best for this technique. Complex stitches can make too many holes in the paper. The technique is used here to decorate the edges of envelopes. The pattern has been further embellished by colouring in with felt tip pens. Needles dull quickly on paper so be prepared.

 Change the top or bobbin tension to create colour mixing of threads

 Hand lace other threads or materials through the stitched pattern

 Lay down strips of fabric or thread and stitch over them.

 Use automatic stitches for appliqué.

◄ 4-4 Automatic zigzag stitch creates a chicken-track effect when a transparent mono filament thread is threaded in the top of the machine. By winding the bobbin with a coloured machine embroidery thread, top and bobbin tensions can be adjusted such that small flecks of bobbin colour will be visible on the surface of the fabric. These little random flecks of colour can add interest to any fabric.

FRAMING FABRIC FOR FREE MACHINING

Free machining within a frame is best suited to developing circular areas of stitchery, but it is necessary to use a frame to secure fabrics that are insufficiently stiff for free machining. To frame your fabric, place the outer ring on a firm, flat surface. Lay the fabric over the ring and press the inner ring into the outer ring, pressing the fabric down between the rings. Stretch the fabric taut by gently pulling and stretching it around the ring. If necessary, tighten the tension screw on the outer ring. Press the inner ring slightly below the outer one to ensure that the fabric will be in close contact with the needle plate.

FREE MACHINING WITHOUT A FRAME

Very stiff fabrics may sometimes be free machined without a frame. Fabrics usually suitable for stitching without frames include pelmet Vilene, Timtex, and lighter fabrics that have been layered or otherwise stiffened with any of the various interfacing materials. It is advisable to use the darning foot to ensure that you do not stitch your fingers along with the fabric. Allow an extra margin when preparing the fabric in the usual way (see page 40). If the fabric is layered, make sure that the layers have been basted together adequately.

▶ 4-5 *Bird Sampler* 16 x 20 cm (6 x 8") - This structure contains bird motifs and borders whose design source is the Book of Kells. Calico (muslin) was painted using acrylic paints. The calico was laid over pelmet vilene with free running stitch worked in some of the areas both as a line stitch and as a filling stitch. The straight lines were stitched with the feed dogs up. *Sallie Miller*

It is easier to develop meandering line possibilities when working without a frame. Be conscious of moving from the top to bottom of the fabric with determined entry and exit points. When the end of the row is reached, lift the presser foot and reverse ends of the fabric. Stitch again, from top to bottom. The textural line sampler (see page 77) is a good example of the exit and entry strategy. Use your fingers to support the fabric while stitching.

Continually move your hands to keep them within close proximity of the stitching. Use your finger strength to keep the fabric taut (this replaces the need

for the frame) and keep them moving. Limp hands are ineffective. Try different fabrics and layering methods to find the one that works best for you. Beginners should start on pelmet vilene (Timtex) to gain experience.

FREE MACHINE EMBROIDERY

Most free machine embroidery is accomplished with two basic stitches - running stitch and zigzag. The fabric should be mounted in a frame or sufficiently stiffened to allow it to be moved about while stitching is applied. It may take considerable practice to get foot and hand working together in co-ordination, creating an even stitch length. This is one technique where the greater the amount of practice put in, the better will be the results produced.

STITCH PATTERNS

To begin, set the stitch length at '0', to stop the feed dogs from moving unnecessarily, and set the stitch width at '0'. Fix a darning foot to the presser bar. The patterns now formed on the fabric will be the direct result of your hands pushing the fabric around

under the needle. Some of the patterns may be quite random, but early embroiderers worked out certain pleasing patterns and gave them names, many of which are still in use. One of the earliest books (from the 1930s and 1940s) by machine embroidery pioneer, Dorothy Benson, used the following names.

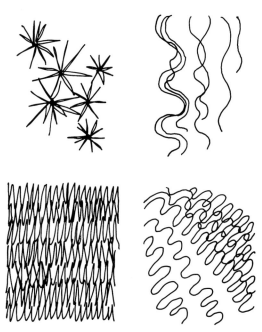

◀◀ 4-6 Free Running Stitch Patterns

A - Vermicelli stitch is used for filling background areas - series of convoluted curves that may be worked in different scales in different areas.

B - Series of interlocking circles.

C - Free running stitch used to first outline a shape, and then to fill the area using encroaching rows from top to bottom.

D - Free running stitch worked from the centre. Start with a simple shape, and in ever enlarging replications of the shape, work to the edges of the area.

◀ 4-7 Free Running Stitch Patterns - Granite/Seed Stitch

A - Free running stitch lines defining shapes are worked first. Two of the shapes are filled with granite stitch worked in circular fashion very close together.

B - Granite stitch is worked in slightly overlapping rows from right to left then left to right.

C - Granite stitch worked from the centre outwards in a continuously enlarging spiral.

D - A few shapes are first defined with running stitch. Granite stitch is then worked around the shapes.

◀ 4-8 Free Running Stitch Patterns

A - Star patterns are made in a continuous line without stopping and starting at each arm.

B - Vertical curving lines are made by stitching from top to bottom and back to top.

C - Stitch pattern is created by moving the fabric up and down across the area in horizontal rows.

D - Looping lines are easy to work either independently or linked to others.

▶ 4-9 Free Zigzag Patterns
A - Zigzag stitch width is set and pattern worked from top to bottom and back to top. Stitch width may be varied while stitching or from row to row.
B - Zigzag stitch width is set and lines radiate from a central point outwards.
C - The lighter shaded area shows zigzag worked from top to bottom in vertical rows. The denser area shows zigzag worked horizontally over the vertical rows. This is a good effect for shading.
D - Zigzag stitch width is set and the rows are worked from left to right and right to left, and from top to bottom.

▶▶4-10 Free Zigzag Patterns
A - Satin stitch is created by moving the fabric or frame very slowly allowing the stitch to build up very tightly together. Stitch width is set.
B - Free satin stitch may be padded by laying down lengths of wool and stitching over the top.
C - A combination of free running stitch patterns. Lay two straight lines and practise aiming for them while making an even pattern, or work letters of the alphabet.
D - Free running stitch patterns into straight lines.

▶ 4-11 Colour Study - Working free running stitch in straight lines, as for hatching, and changing thread colours from time to time, will produce some interesting plays of colour on the fabric.

VERMICELLI

Visualize a plate of vermicelli pasta, and it becomes clear how this stitch got its name. An alternative name is crazy stitch. The squiggly pattern, worked with free running stitch, takes great care and practice, but it serves as a wonderful background pattern with which to cover open areas of fabric.

GRANITE/SEED

This stitch is formed by overlapping circles. Circles may be tiny and dense, or may be large and open, exposing the background fabric.

Working with free running stitch offers one total control over stitching lines or patterns. Some of the most exciting results are gained with one or more of the following techniques: quilting, layering, appliqué, fabric painting and lace. Pay careful attention to the unlimited tones and shades of thread colour that may be used. Effective colour combinations can bring a zingy dimensional effect.

FREE ZIGZAG STITCH

Free zigzag is achieved in the same way as free running

stitch , but with the exception that the stitch width is set on the machine. While machining, move the frame more slowly than for free running stitch. Increase foot pressure on the pedal (speeding up the stitching) to create satin stitch. The fabric may be moved in any direction under the needle.

▲ 4-18 Free satin stitch worked while changing stitch width during the stitching.

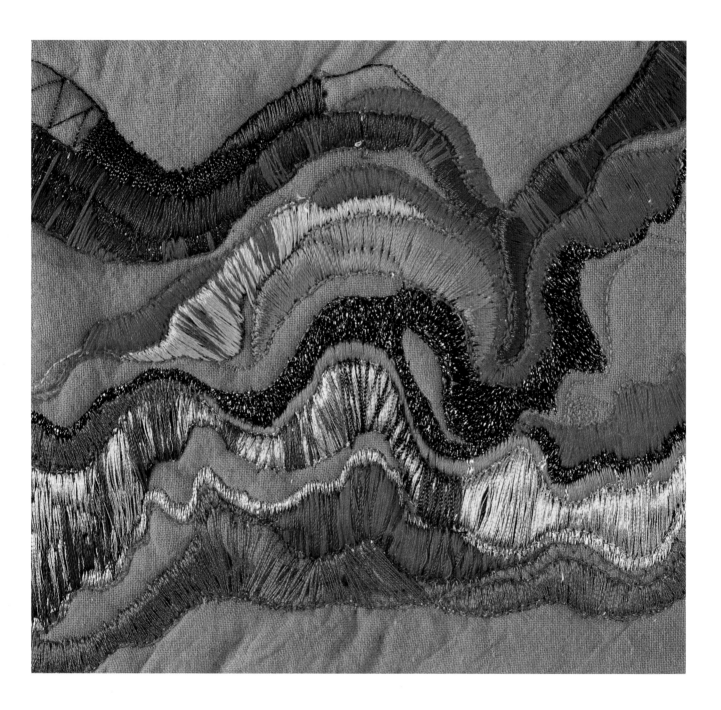

▲ 4-19 Work free satin stitch in a frame using the widest stitch width. Work slowly, shifting the frame to obtain as wide a stitch as desired.

QUILTING WITH AUTOMATIC STITCHES

Machine quilting may be accomplished with straight stitch, zigzag, satin stitch, or almost any other decorative stitch. Automatic straight stitch is excellent for sewing straight lines across the quilt; on small, intricate designs, however, complex curving lines may prove difficult to stitch in automatic mode.

When straight stitch is used, the stitch must be

◄ 4-12 White Diamonds - Machine quilting using straight stitch and narrow satin stitch. Length of the first diamond is about 2 cm (³/₄").

lengthened to accommodate the additional thickness of any batting that may be used. If the stitch is not lengthened to take account of the batting, the work may buckle or pucker under the thread tension. A useful way of experimenting with automatic quilting is to make a sampler on a grid of layered fabrics, such as the Continuous Stitch Star Sampler, Sun Motif Sampler, and Manipulated Fabric Sampler on pages 87-94. The basic machine set-up for automatic quilting is as given below, though details such as the stitch length will vary according to the exact nature of the quilting.

REQUIREMENTS

THREADS

Use machine embroidery threads for decorative effects. For strength, use quilting or dressmakers' thread.

FOOT

Use the general sewing presser foot or other appropriate foot (a transparent foot makes it easier to see the build-up of stitches).

MACHINE

Set the machine at the appropriate settings for the stitch or technique in use.

STITCH LENGTH

If straight stitch is being used, set the stitch length to between 3 and 3.5 mm (¹/₈") to compensate for the thickness of the layers.

MACHINE QUILTING IN FREE MODE

Quilting in this sense refers to working with more than one layer of fabric. Quilting complex patterns and tight circular curves pose even greater problems for machine embroiderers than normal machine quilting. It can be very difficult to machine in the normal automatic mode while turning and manipulating a piece with layers of backing fabric and batting. In practical terms, it may prove nigh on impossible.

The solution is for the machine embroiderer to switch to free running stitch. With the feed dogs retracted, the fabric may be manipulated by hand under the needle. The hands take the place of an embroidery frame in supporting the fabric under the needle. With a little practice, the co-ordination of sewing speed (foot) and hand movement will produce smooth, even stitch production. Since the fabric may be moved in any direction, very complex patterns and lines may be produced with considerable dexterity and evenness of stitch.

COUCHED THREADS USING AUTOMATIC STITCHES

Couching is the process whereby threads are laid on the surface of a fabric and held down by stitches made with another thread. The couched thread is the thread that is laid on the surface of the fabric. The couching thread is the thread used to secure the couched thread to the background.

REQUIREMENTS

FABRICS

Heavier weights of fabric usually work best with couching. Recommended materials include heavyweight Pellon/vilene/Timtex, velvet/velveteen with backing, denim, heavyweight upholstery fabric, layered fabrics and paper. The suggested fabrics are relatively stiff and therefore will not drape very well, but they resist puckering under the pressure of a large quantity of threads worked on the surface.

There are occasions when a background fabric of a lighter weight is desirable. You will often need to give these a bit of extra stiffening before you apply stitching. Try interfacing or stitch-and-tear as a backing.

COUCHED THREADS

The couched thread is usually of a type that would prove difficult to pass through the fabric in the usual machine embroidery fashion. Almost any type of thread or cord may be couched, ranging from woolly, wiry, bulky or delicate threads to some very unusual materials, such as leather thongs, piping cord, satin-stitched cords, hand-made cords or ribbons.

COUCHING THREADS

Use either machine embroidery or standard dressmakers' thread. Some unusual colour effects are created when a thread of one colour is stitched over a thread of a second colour. A quick test on a sample will indicate the effects of combining any two or more colours.

FOOT

A clear plastic foot is very handy for this kind of stitching, as it is a great advantage to be able to see the stitches as they are applied. As an alternative, the open-toed appliqué foot, shorter than the standard foot, is handy.

STITCHES

Any stitch that is formed by the side-to-side movement of the needle is suitable. These include zigzag, satin stitch, and most of the decorative/utility/embroidery stitches available on the majority of modern machines. Adjust the stitch width so that the stitch is just wide enough to cover the couched thread without piercing it. Avoid complex embroidery/decorative stitches in which the feed dogs move the fabric back and forth while stitching. Ensure that you are not trying to couch down a thread that is wider than the widest stitch width setting on your machine.

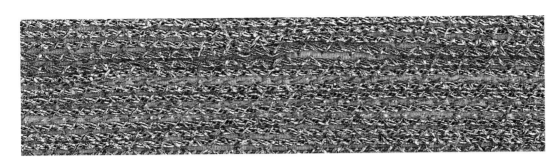

◀ 4-13 Automatic stitching of couched threads
A - Gold wiry threads and thin cords are laid side by side and couched using zigzag stitch.

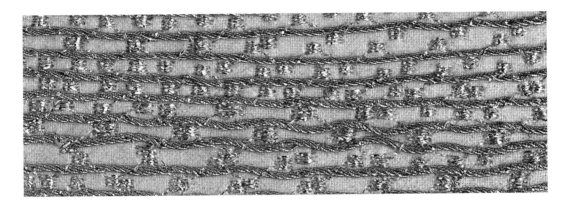

◀ 4-13B A programmed decorative stitch that creates small satin stitch blobs on either side of the couched thread was used. The machine's top thread was metallic machine embroidery thread.

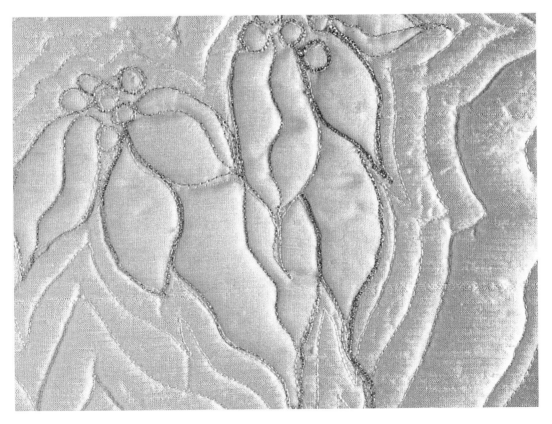

◀ 4-13C Free machine quilting on silk fabric echoes the shape of the leaves. A lightweight batting is used between the silk top fabric and the organza lining.

▶ 4-14 Free machining of couched threads - An assortment of thread types, including knitting wool, strips of net, lamé, and other fabric were couched to a background fabric using free running stitch.

STARTING AND FINISHING

Before beginning to stitch in the chosen decorative pattern, make a few straight stitches forward and then reverse back to the start, alongside the couched thread. When you have done this, change from straight stitch to the decorative stitch pattern. If you have a problem getting good coverage over the couched thread, or if it is difficult to follow the guidelines, try using a transparent thread, such as nylon filament, to baste down the couched thread. Apply the nylon with a basic zigzag stitch, and then return to your decorative thread and work over the top of the transparent nylon. The nylon thread will not be visible when the work is finished. Alternatively, the couched thread can be basted to the background fabric by hand before you begin machine stitching.

If you find that the fabric is not moving forward as stitching begins, try increasing the stitch length. If that still does not correct the problem, check to see that the couched thread is not too thick to pass easily under the presser foot.

When starting up, leave a tail of couched thread, 7.5 to 10 cm (3 to 4″) long, at the beginning of each row. The tail provides a useful finger-hold with which to help control the start of stitching. Begin the stitching about 4 to 5 cm (1½ to 2″) in from the edge of the fabric.

To finish, use a stiletto or large needle to make a hole big enough to allow the couched thread to pass through. Make a loop in a length of sewing thread and pass the loop end through the eye of a needle. Catch the couched thread in the loop and pass the needle through the hole, pulling the tail of the couched thread through to the back of the fabric. Either secure the tails, by tying them off or stitching them to the back of the fabric, or leave them hanging over the edge to serve as a fringe.

COUCHING WITH FREE MACHINING

Free machining techniques can easily be used to couch threads. These may be arranged in loops or other

designs and may be of any length. Almost any type of thread can be used, as with automatic stitching. The (top) sewing thread is not intended to be seen and should therefore be the same colour as the couched thread. The bobbin thread may be any thread of your choice. Use free running stitch or free zigzag, and either use your darning foot or sew without a foot. The background fabric should be framed for this technique unless it is stiffened through layering.

Step 1

Form a loop of the thread that is to be couched. With your left index finger, hold the loop on the top fabric and stitch over the protruding ends. Continue this process, forming loops as required.

Step 2

This is not continuous stitching, but a start-stop process as each loop is individually formed and attached. Make small stitches over the edges of the couched thread. To achieve an even coverage, it is important to ensure that the loops are close together. Loops may either be left as they are or clipped to create a fringe.

CABLE STITCH WITH FEED DOGS UP

Cable stitch resembles a hand-couched thread worked on top of the fabric. The stitch is made with the underside of the fabric facing up and the right side facing down over the feed dogs. Since the stitch is in effect worked face down, the design may be drawn directly on the reverse side of the fabric, as this is the side you will be looking at while you stitch. Gently flowing lines and simple geometric patterns can be stitched using this technique. Machine cable stitch has the advantage of showing up well on some quilted or piled fabrics where other stitches might sink in and disappear. The stitch is formed in standard machine lockstitching fashion. The only difference is that the thread wound on the bobbin will be of heavier gauge than ordinary sewing thread.

REQUIREMENTS

FABRICS

Try using heavyweight cotton, wool, silk, velvet, uphol-stery fabric, or, perhaps, felt, paper or organza. If the fabric selected for this technique is insufficiently heavy to support the stitching, interfacing may be used to make it more firm.

BOBBIN THREAD

The bobbin (feature) thread may be perlé, six-strand-ed cotton, crochet cotton or try a more unusual thread, perhaps a metallic.

TOP THREAD

Thread the top of the machine with dressmakers' or machine embroidery thread. If it is desirable for the top thread to be unseen, a mono-filament (transpar-ent) thread could be used.

NEEDLE

Begin with a size 90 (14), changing it only if it is necessary to use one better suited to the particular conditions.

FOOT

Use the general sewing presser foot.

STITCH LENGTH

Normal stitch length is generally satisfactory, but experiment for different effects.

TOP AND BOBBIN TENSIONS

The top tension may not require any tension adjustment from normal, but for most heavy threads, the bobbin will normally require some easing (loosening) of tension. This will enable the thicker thread to spool off the bobbin at about the same tension as a normal sewing thread. For a loose, looping stitch, the bobbin tension may be set very low. Some machines have a special tension bypass for thicker threads. It is important to read the manual for your machine to discover which tension adjustments are possible and how to make them.

STITCHES

Straight stitch is the most usual choice for this tech-nique, but once you have practised with straight stitch you will discover that other decorative stitches may be used for cable stitch. The most suitable of the decora-tive stitches for this purpose are those that develop in a straight, forward moving line, rather than through widely variable forward and backward movements. When cable stitching, you may find that some decora-tive stitches require an even lower bobbin tension than cabling with straight stitch.

STITCHING

Try to wind the bobbin evenly and do not let it get overloaded with the heavier thread. Before you com-mence stitching, wind a few spare bobbins with the heavier thread. Since the bobbin will not hold as much as it would when wound with normal sewing thread, it will quickly run out of thread.

It is impossible to watch the stitches form on the underside of the fabric, so it is good practice to try a test piece to ensure that the technique will work sat-isfactorily with the fabric and threads chosen, and to provide an opportunity to make adjustments.

To begin, place the right side of the fabric face down on the bed of the machine, over the feed dogs. Bring the bobbin thread to the surface of the fabric. If for any rea-son it is difficult to do this, make a small hole with a large

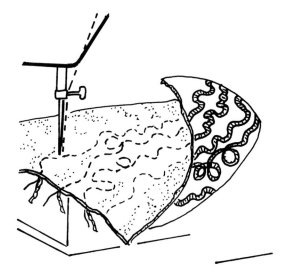

▶ 4-15 Free cable stitch - This stitch is worked from the wrong side of the fabric since the heavy (couched) thread is pulled up from the bobbin. Almost any pattern could be produced through movement of the fabric under the needle.

needle or stiletto and ease the thread through by hand. The bobbin thread should lie neatly, with a tight interlocking stitch securing it to the fabric. Do not back stitch.

To finish, again, do not make a back stitch at the end of the line of stitches, as you would with normal sewing. Instead, use a hand sewing needle to bring the tail of the bobbin thread up to the wrong side of the fabric. Tie this off by hand.

CABLE STITCH USING FREE MACHINE MODE

Free cable stitch is used to create a high relief, three-dimensional, textured build-up of heavy threads on fabric. If you work with an embroidery frame, you will be able to use many fabrics that it would not otherwise be possible to machine. The threads, top and bobbin tensions, needles, and hints needed for this technique are all virtually identical with those already listed for use with automatic cable stitch. Stitching in the free mode with the feed dogs down, however, allows the embroiderer to execute much more intricate, intuitive patterns, tight curves, and circular and organic shapes.

REQUIREMENTS

FRAMED STITCHING
If fabric to be machined is mounted in an embroidery frame, more exact hand motions will be possible when the fabric is under positive control. The frame will also help guard against puckering caused by dense stitching.

STITCHING WITHOUT A FRAME
It is possible to stitch heavier fabric without first mounting it in a frame; for a lighter fabric, you can choose to work without a frame if you stiffen the embroidery fabric by backing it with interfacing or layering it with other fabrics.

FOOT
Ensure that the presser bar is in the down position. If it is difficult to stitch without a foot, use the darning foot supplied with your machine, or use a spring needle.

STITCHING

Set your stitch length to '0', as usual when free machining. Bring the bobbin thread up through the fabric in the same way as described for cable stitching in the automatic mode. Take a few small stitches in place to secure the threads. It is advisable to stop for a moment and trim away tails of threads. They will undoubtedly get in the way while stitching.

To finish, take a few small stitches to secure the threads, as at the beginning.

MACHINE-WRAPPED CORDS

Colourful satin-stitched cord, with a wide range of embroidery uses, can be produced by this simple technique in which a base or core thread is covered in the chosen thread.

REQUIREMENTS

CORE THREAD
This may be piping cord, string or wool.

WRAPPING THREAD
Use machine embroidery threads for the top and bobbin threads. Both threads should be the same colour if a single colour of cord is desired. Some machine types dislike rayon threads on the top of the machine as these can be slippery and constant breakage of thread may be a problem.

FOOT
Use a darning foot or no foot at all. Some machines have a knitting overlock foot, which will channel the cord while you are stitching over it. The machine should still be used in the free machining mode.

TOP AND BOBBIN TENSIONS
Decrease (loosen) the top tension if it is set for general sewing. For a smooth cord, the bobbin tension should be increased slightly.

WRAPPING

Set the machine for wide zigzag stitch (the needle should span the cord without piercing it). Use free machine settings, with the feed dogs down and the stitch length at '0'.

Hold the core thread tautly under the foot (one hand behind needle, the other in front). Begin machining, feeding the cord towards the back of the machine, away from you. The rate at which the cord is fed through the machine will determine the stitch length, and hence the coverage of the cord. The cord may be moved forwards and backwards to get even or uneven coverage as desired. It is important to hold the cord flat down on the bed of the machine while stitching. The threads should lock on the underside of the cord, allowing the top thread to wrap completely around the cord.

If you find that you have a problem with constant thread breakage, try using a cotton thread of a matching colour in the bobbin and loosen the top tension slightly.

MACHINE LACE

A multitude of different patterns may be used to create machine lace, free running stitch being used for most of them. Free zigzag stitch can also be used, but ensure that lines of stitching intersect each other so that the zigzag does not unravel. Threads must criss-cross to create a supporting network. Heavier lace may be produced by retracing the stitch lines many times.

It is useful to work out ideas for patterns and locate where spaces will be before stitching begins. Try drawing patterns on paper in continuous lines without lifting the pencil. Stitch patterns may be circular, granite stitch, or encroaching line stitches. (Make sure that threads intersect each other.) Open effects may be eliminated by applying a dense network of stitches, similar to the creation of a threadlike fabric.

Use one of the disappearing fabric products to support the stitchery, setting the fabric in a frame. Choose a needle to suit the fabric, and experiment with various threads, making samples before committing yourself to a finished piece.

You can wind your bobbins with perlé (pearl) cotton or six-stranded cotton and make cable stitch lace. This technique will create a heavier lace than the free-machined varietys.

4-17 Machine lace - The star with the tassel was worked on hot water soluble fabric. The 10-pointed star is actually two overlapping 5-pointed stars. Lace is appliquéd over the star.

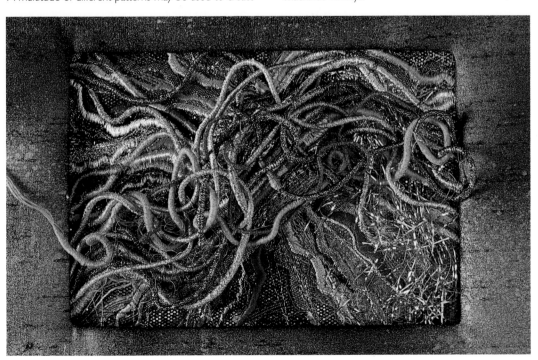

4-16 *Polynesian Sunrise* 15 x 20 cm (6 x 8″) The background fabric was appliquéd using satin stitch. The central form was padded from the back. A profusion of satin stitch cords were entwined and built up over the surface.

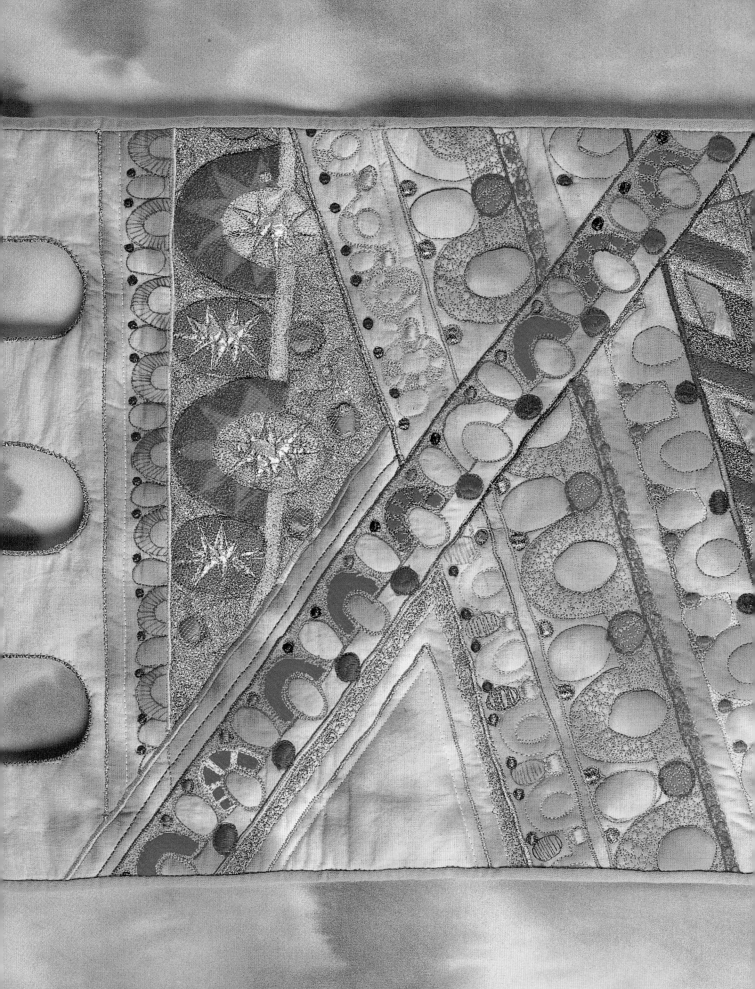

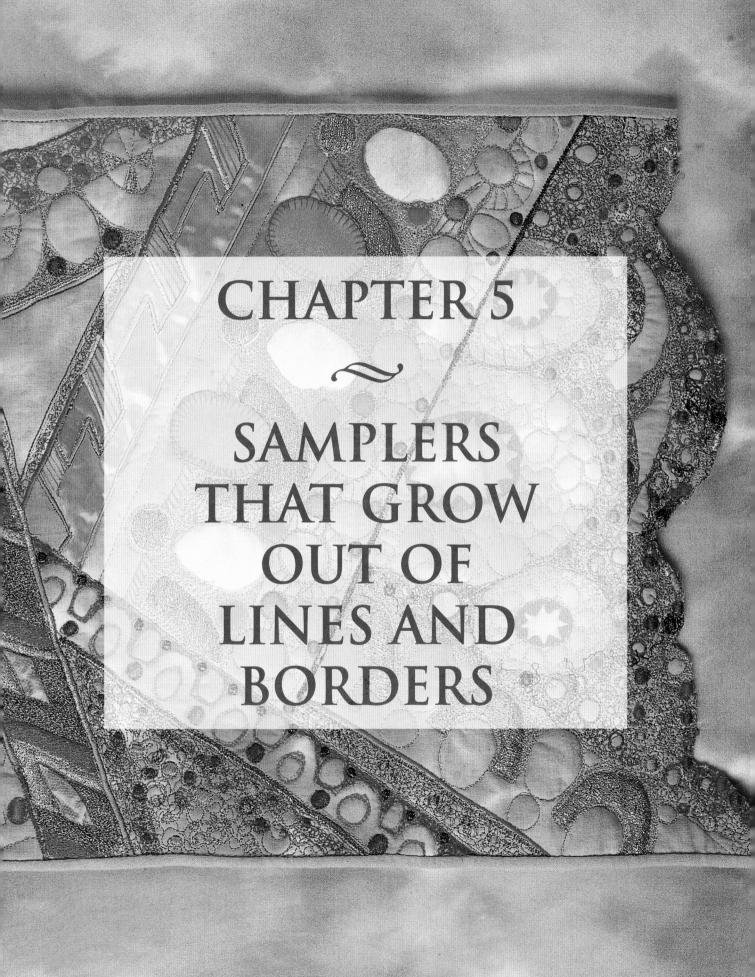

CHAPTER 5

~

SAMPLERS THAT GROW OUT OF LINES AND BORDERS

THE FOLLOWING EXERCISES are intended to get aspiring machine embroiderers past the 'I can't do it stage' which can afflict even those who have read all the books. Many of the stitch samplers seen here are basic design concepts. Lines and borders provide a simple structure upon which to place a variety of patterns, and it is fun to experiment with different stitch types. Some samplers, such as the Textural Line Sampler, evolve from one line. The line I like to call 'the quivering line' is a good example with which to practise organic shapes, but most of the samplers featured use more than one method of working.

The actual working of a sampler gives one invaluable time on the job. This hands-on work is an essential step on the road to mastering skills and patience, as well as gaining confidence in controlling the needle while stitching lines, scribbles, and patterns.

The visual impact of stitches and techniques can act as a spur to creative thoughts in most students. The time and effort required to make one small sampler using multi-stitches and steps can be a startling revelation to some. Knowing when there is just enough stitching and/or colour on a sampler for maximum impact and effect is a skill that comes with much practical work. While many machine-embroidered designs may look abstract, there must still be an underlying structure if they are to have artistic appeal. That structure may, after much work, seem to disappear.

Many stitchers may at first be tempted to consider samplers a waste of time and effort, especially if no obvious product emerges. Samplers, however, can play a very important role in conquering machine embroidery techniques.

The samplers described here are complete with instructions and guide lines, but it is not the intention of the author for people to feel the need to slavishly duplicate any of the works shown. The actual stitching of the samplers is intended to expand knowledge and develop creative skills. Use the samplers as building blocks, or as vocabularies of stitches and techniques for a myriad of new creations.

All samplers are based upon the initial work of preparation described on page 40. The sizes given are the finished sizes, but you should always cut fabric with an all around border of 4 to 5 cm (1½ to 2˝) larger than the finished size.

Some ideas have been included about ways in which to finish samplers (see pages 102-105). The finishing treatment can turn a sampler into a completed work of machine embroidery and greatly increases its appeal. Spread throughout this chapter are photographs of other people's work, as an added inspiration to the possibilities that may lie beyond the sampler.

LACED THREAD SAMPLER

Straight stitch was developed to stitch seams together, but this basic stitch may also be used as a foundation for combining hand embroidery stitches with machine stitching. The machine stitches may be applied in parallel lines, like railway tracks, or they may bend and turn, perhaps with a variable space between lines of stitches, or in combinations of double, triple or almost any number of lines. Thick, colourful, metallic or other threads of character can then be interlaced through the straight stitch, either singly or in any combination of multiple threads.

This technique can become quite addictive since it very quickly produces easily worked yet beautiful combinations and patterns. Refer to books on hand embroidery for further ideas on composite stitches.

REQUIREMENTS

FABRIC

You can use almost any firm fabric, such as cotton twill or quilting cotton 13 x 18 cm (5½ x 7˝), including allowances.

BACKING

Use either iron-on interfacing or a tear-away paper backing.

MACHINE THREAD

Use a strong thread, such as dressmakers' or quilting

◀◀ 5-1 *Moons over Mexico - Wall Hanging - 28 x 61 cm (11 x 24˝). Techniques - Appliqué, free machine embroidery, and automatic machine embroidery. The design is a repetition of two repeating motifs. The scale of the borders and motifs changes throughout the piece.*

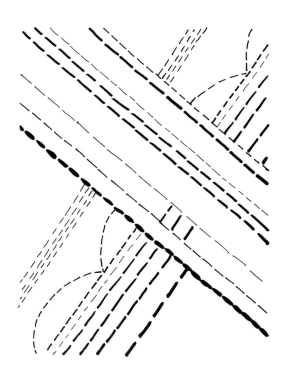

◀◀ 5-2 *Laced Thread Sampler*
Diagram indicates placement of straight stitches in preparation for lacing.

◀ 5-3 *Laced Thread Sampler*
Size - 13 x 18 cm (5 x 7") A variety of different hand and machine embroidery threads are used for interlacing.

cotton, that will stand up to the rigours of the lacing. Use the same thread in the bobbin as for the top.

NEEDLE

Use a needle that will allow easy passage of the thread through the eye, such as a size 90 (14).

LACING THREAD

Experiment with a range of threads, including cotton,

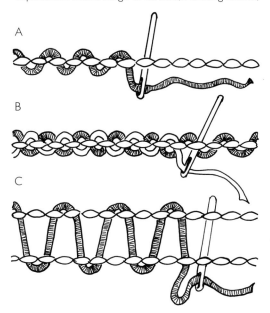

A

B

C

silk or metallic hand embroidery threads, wool yarns, and even thin ribbons.

LACING TOOL

Use a blunt-pointed tapestry needle to lace the decorative threads through the machine stitches.

MACHINE

Set the machine for automatic stitching (feed dogs up).

FOOT

Use the satin foot or the embroidery foot

MACHINE STITCHES

Use the automatic straight stitch – if the machine has the capability, try sewing a double straight stitch (this makes the work stronger). Zigzag or some other simple decorative stitch will provide more alternative lacing patterns.

STITCH LENGTH

The stitch length must be adjusted to allow passage of the lacing thread and needle between stitches - for straight stitch, try 3.5 mm (about seven stitches per inch).

◀ 5-4 Diagram indicates lacing stitches:
A. Threaded backstitch.
B. Threaded back stitch - identical to the preceding, but a second thread is laced through the vacant areas taking on the appearance of a repeating "8".
C. Thread is laced between 2 rows of machine stitching.

DECORATIVE STITCH SAMPLER

To find the ideal stitch pattern for a waistcoat that Fay Twydell wanted to create for her grandson, she stitched samples of a wide variety of stitches that might suit her need. This was also a good test to determine the type of fabric that would support the stitches and create the effect she had in mind. It was also important to make samples to find out how the stitches would look when worked in parallel rows, especially as she wanted the stitches to lie flat without puckering the fabric. The samples helped her to choose the final look and feeling of her project. If you wish to make a similar waistcoat, you will need the items listed below, together with a simple commercial pattern for the basic garment. You can then add whatever decoration you choose to the pattern pieces.

CHILD'S WAISTCOAT

Baste medium-weight interfacing to the background fabric. This will make the fabric sufficiently heavy to withstand the stitchery. The thickness also creates a soft rippling effect on the fabric between the rows of stitches. Fusible interfacing was tested, but was found to make the fabric too stiff for the purpose.

Separate the paper pattern pieces and lay them on the fabric, allowing about 5 cm (2″) of fabric around the edges. Draw around the outline of each pattern piece on the fabric, but do not cut out the pattern at this point. Find the longitudinal centre of each pattern piece and stitch along this line first. Then, working from each side of the centre line, stitch a parallel row. Begin and end each row of stitching about 2.5 cm (1″) past the traced outline of the pattern (this avoids the need to backstitch at the end of each row). At the finish of each row, turn the fabric and stitch another parallel row back in the opposite direction. The alternation of stitch direction prevents distortion of the fabric.

When you have finished all the decorative stitching, lay out the decorated fabric and replace the pat-

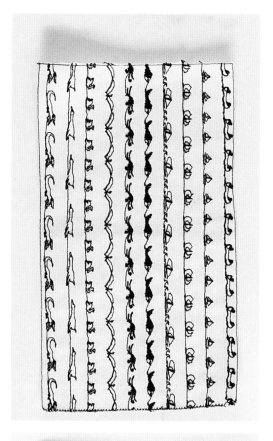

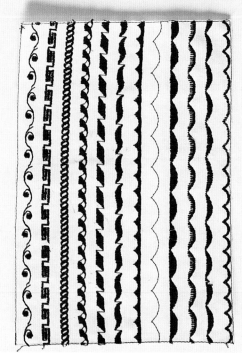

tern over the fabric. It will now be apparent that the stitching has caused the fabric to contract, making the pattern outlines smaller than those of the original pattern pieces (part of the reason for the allowance around pattern pieces). Redraw the pattern on the fabric and stitch around the final pattern markings. Cut out pattern pieces outside the stitched lines. Stitch the pattern together following the pattern instructions.

REQUIREMENTS

FABRICS
Approximately 30 × 35 cm (12 × 14″) of pure cotton twill was used for the main fabric, interfaced with a sew-in (Vilene/Pellon) interfacing.

THREADS
Select a few spools of machine embroidery threads, in a variety of shades and thickness. Stitch samples will indicate that thinner, finer threads will work best for stitch patterns that are packed very tightly together.

NEEDLE
Use a size 90 (14) needle unless you find that another needle is more suitable for the thread and fabric type.

STITCH PATTERNS

One pitfall to avoid is an excessive variety of stitches. As they first begin to use decorative stitches in a creative way, embroiderers new to machine embroidery often have a tendency to combine too many stitches on a single work. This will almost always result in a confused appearance.

Notice that only two stitch patterns were used here. The appearance of these two stitches was significantly varied through the use of the stitch length and stitch width controls on the machine. This helped to give a more three-dimensional effect to the fabric and stitches. Rows were intentionally spaced irregularly to add to this effect.

Stitch patterns worked back-to-back created an illusion of additional patterns, and an attempt to find a good balance of colours and tones was made when planning the stitches.

Time spent making samples to test ideas is essential to the success of a project such as this. In this case, Fay Twydell spent six hours making samples and three hours on the stitchery and make-up of the waistcoat itself. The time spent on sampling – double the time taken to make the article – assured the artist of success with the finished work.

RIBBON SAMPLER

The design basis for this sample is an arrangement of areas generated by dividing the whole shape with ribbons. The resulting fabric has a soft draping nature that is suitable for quilt squares, waistcoats, jackets, or wall hangings. Try your own design on paper as an aid to finding a pleasing starting point. The step drawings show a slightly simplified version of the finished embroidery; for those who are experimenting with this technique for the first time, it is a good idea to keep the paper design simple.

The example seen here is based on an arrangement of six rows of triangles, each row of a different size and each arranged above, below, or through a length of ribbon. Ribbons are used as a guide when stitching the rows, but the triangles are not worked in a precise geometric pattern. Let the design grow freely.

APPLYING RIBBON BY HAND

If you choose to apply the ribbons to the fabric by hand using slip stitch (see step 2) you will find it simpler to ease them into the correct positions and avoid the puckering that may occur with machine stitching when stitching on the bias. The woven edges of ribbons can be quite firm and unyielding. For best results ensure that the background fabric is of the same weight as the ribbon or slightly heavier, and baste the ribbons in position by hand.

APPLYING RIBBON BY MACHINE

If you elect to stitch the ribbons in place by machine instead of hand basting them, the following tips will help you to create a successful sampler.

 Either lay the ribbons from selvage to selvage on the background fabric, rather than across the bias, or reduce the size of the sampler to about half the size of the one shown here, which measures 33 x 45 cm (13 x 18″).

 Use straight stitch or zigzag to attach ribbons.

 Try to work out an even distribution of ribbons and stitches across the fabric.

 Move from one area to the next to ensure even working of each area.

 If the fabric begins to pucker during stitching, lay a piece of tear-away stabilizer under the fabric before placing it under the machine needle. Do not baste the added stabilizer to the fabric.

REQUIREMENTS

FABRICS

Approximately 33 x 45 cm (13 x 18″) of a light-to-medium weight of cotton or silk fabric, backed by a thin, natural, or synthetic type of batting (wadding).

THREADS

Use machine embroidery or dressmakers' threads in tones of the selected colours.

COUCHING

Gold braid and cord are couched to ribons for additional interest.

RIBBONS

Use a selection of woven-edge ribbons in widths varying between 3 mm and 4 cm (1/8 and 1 1/2″).

NEEDLE

Use quilting or regular size 80 (12) or 90 (14).

Step 1

Baste the two layers of fabric together. The success of this technique depends upon good basting of the two fabrics. Leave a border of 4 to 5 cm (1 1/2 to 2″) outside the estimated finished area of the sampler.

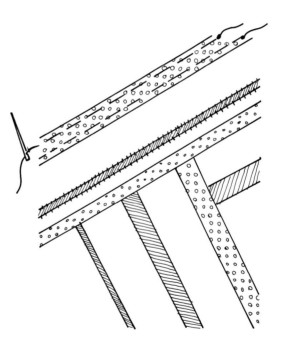

◀ 5-9 - Step 1

Step 2

Use ribbons of differing widths to divide the sampler space. Move the ribbons over the surface until a pleasing arrangement has been created. Pin and hand baste the ribbons in place. The basted ribbons can either be secured by hand, using slip stitch, or with the machine, by straight-stitching along each ribbon edge.

▶ 5-10 Step 3

▶▶ 5-11 Step 4

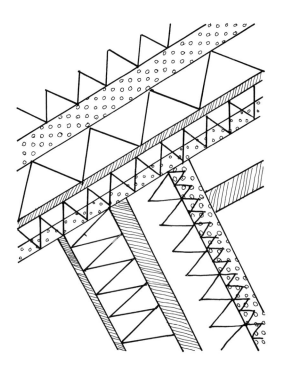

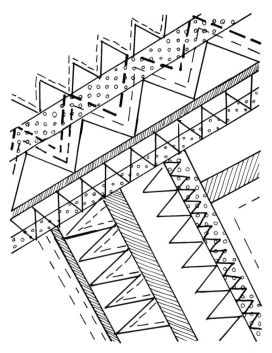

Step 3

Using the ribbons as guidelines, mark out rows of triangles with dressmakers' chalk or a light marking pencil and ruler. Make automatic straight stitch along these lines to quilt the fabric.

Step 4

Using automatic stitch mode, follow the lines of the previously created triangles as you like. Make as many lines as pleases the eye. Choose a few areas for machine-couched highlights. Over these areas, use zigzag stitch to apply cord or braid. On the sample, gold braid was used for the accent thread.

TECHNIQUES

AUTOMATIC MACHINE QUILTING

Thread the machine with machine embroidery or dressmakers' thread. Choose three or four colours only, but try to find different tonal values within each colour. These colours should harmonize closely with the background fabric. Choose a single colour to be used as the accent colour. The accent colour should

contrast with the background colour and be used only for highlighting at the end of the project. Set the machine for automatic stitching, using the standard presser foot and ordinary straight stitch.

▶ 5-8 *Ribbon Sampler* 33 x 46 cm (13 x 18") The basic structure for this piece started with the laying down of ribbons to delineate areas for further stitching. A soft quilted effect has been obtained through hand and machine stitches.

RIBBON APPLIQUÉ

The ribbons are all of a similar colour to the background fabric, but five different widths. Find one fairly wide ribbon along with four narrower ones. The example uses plain satin, sheer and metallic ribbons with dots of various sizes.

The sampler in the photograph uses cut-back appliqué, with sections of ribbon being cut away to accentuate the triangular stitching. If you wish to incorporate this technique into your own sampler, baste the relevant ribbons in place, but do not slip-stitch them to the fabric. Machine embroider the triangle pattern along the ribbon; remove basting stitches, and cut away triangles of fabric.

HAND QUILTING

Hand quilting is optional on this piece. Use the technique that seems most suitable. Hand quilting will provide more contrast of line and add its own interest. Any combination of machine embroidery or hand stitching threads may be used. Use a hand stitching needle, such as a crewel embroidery needle.

MACHINE COUCHING

Use machine couching to add accents to this sampler. For the couched thread, try perlé cotton, cord, ribbon, or round braid. As the couching thread, use machine embroidery thread for both the top and bottom of the machine. Choose a needle to suit the fabric used.

TEXTURAL LINE SAMPLER

Using a very straight-forward method, a richly encrusted fabric can be created. Lines of stitches flow in, around and over each other. From top to bottom, the lines flow and entwine with each other. This creates a feeling of organic movement not unlike that of rivers or the flowing and gentle contours of a beautiful landscape.

This sampler combines a number of different machine embroidery techniques – appliqué, free machine embroidery, free zigzag, free satin and free cable stitch – all in the same piece. No frame is used with this technique. The finished fabric created through this technique is quite stiff and could be used as a wall hanging, cushion cover, bag, collar or cuffs. The sampler featured here took about six hours to stitch.

TIPS FOR SUCCESS

Be sure not to take short cuts with fabric preparation and basting. Allow a full 5 cm (2″) border that will be cut away in the finishing stage. If you feel any uncertainty about how the four dividing lines may appear, try drawing a few paper samples to test the design before committing stitches to fabric. Stitch the central lines first. Notice that the lines are not identical, but they should be in sympathy with each other. Do not be reticent about stitching over previous stitches – allow the sample to develop a life of its own.

REQUIREMENTS

FABRICS

There are four layers of fabric altogether, each approximately 14 × 18 cm (5½ × 7″). The bottom layer is nylon or silk organza, or cotton organdie; the next is thin batting/wadding; this is covered by cotton or silk, and finally there is a top layer of nylon net.

THREADS

Use machine embroidery threads in a large range of colours for most of the stitching, and cotton floss for the free cable stitch.

NEEDLE

Choose a size 80 (12) or 90 (14) embroidery or top-stitch needle, or one that suits the particular stitch to be applied.

FOOT

The machine is set for free machining, so use a darning foot (see page 9).

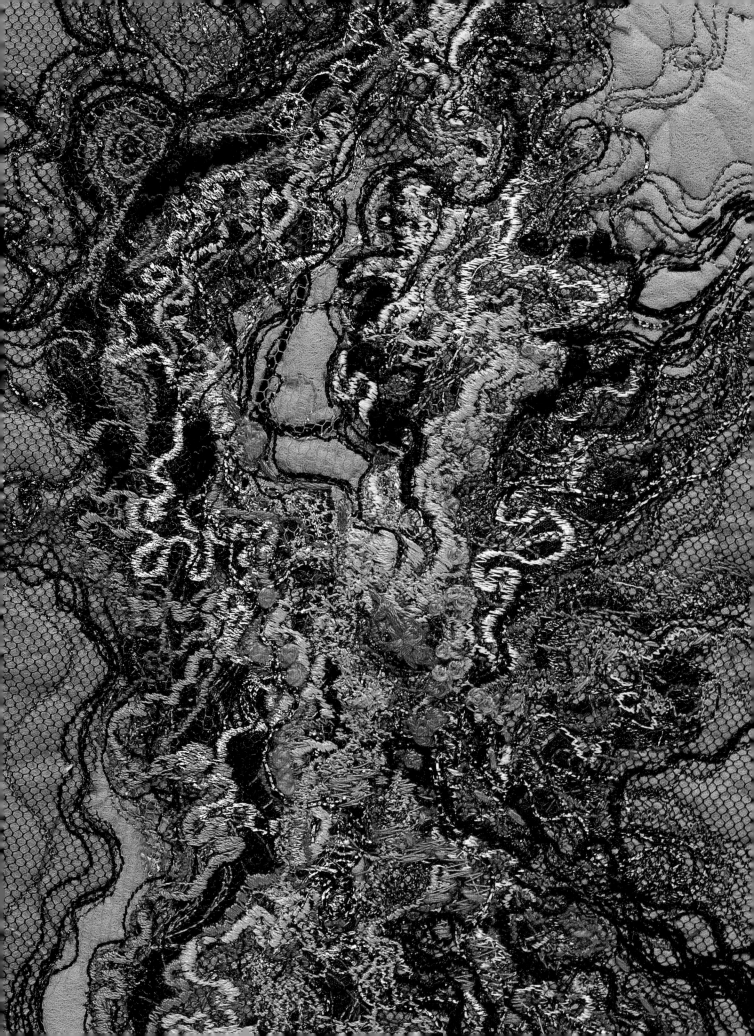

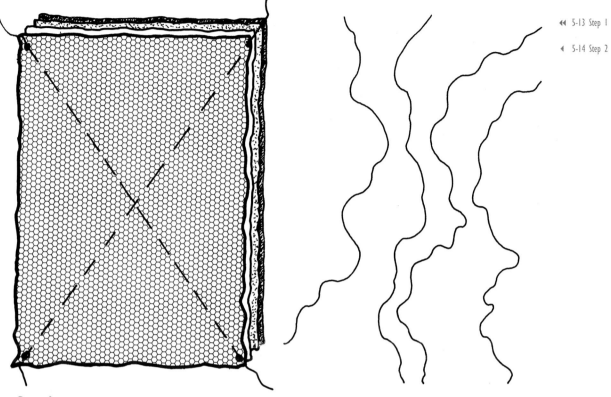

◀◀ 5-13 Step 1

◀ 5-14 Step 2

Step 1

Layer the fabrics in the following order: organza or organdie on the bottom, thin wadding/batting as the second layer, cotton or silk (your choice) as the third layer, and nylon tulle/net as the top layer. Baste all the fabrics together (see page 41).

Step 2

Begin at the top of the sampler and stitch four lines in free running stitch. Stitch from the top to the bottom, using thread of a colour that tones with that of the top fabric. Stitch the lines so as to divide the sampler in an appealing way. The resulting dividing lines will loosely form the base on which the pattern is built.

Step 3

Clip away the net in two of the divided areas, using small, sharp scissors. The result gives the fabric a certain three-dimensional aspect. The more experienced embroiderer may wish to repeat the process, creating more shapes in different colours, and thus increasing complexity and interest through the play of shades and tones.

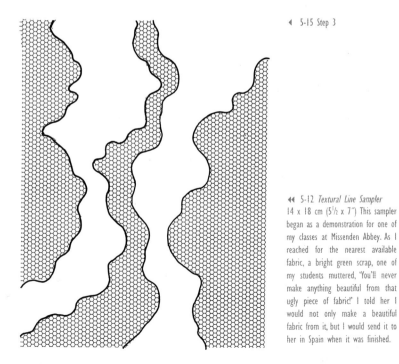

◀ 5-15 Step 3

◀◀ 5-12 *Textural Line Sampler*
14 x 18 cm (5½ x 7″) This sampler began as a demonstration for one of my classes at Missenden Abbey. As I reached for the nearest available fabric, a bright green scrap, one of my students muttered, 'You'll never make anything beautiful from that ugly piece of fabric!' I told her I would not only make a beautiful fabric from it, but I would send it to her in Spain when it was finished.

▶▶ 5-16 Step 4

▶ 5-17 Step 5

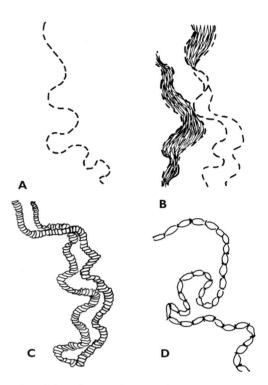

Step 4

Work more lines of free running stitch from top to bottom of the fabric. It is important to ensure that lines run generally top to bottom. There is no need to retrace the exact contour of the preceding lines. In fact, more interest is created if the lines move out and away, and then back alongside each other. Stitch lines in soft curves, occasionally taking a line for a brief meandering stroll across the fabric. Alternate between free running stitch, zigzag and thin satin stitch. Leave some areas with little or no stitching. Concentrate on two or three areas to build up greater stitch density and more heavily encrusted areas. Change top threads frequently to build up a rich variety of colours.

Step 5

Free running stitch creates a very thin, fine line that demands much stitching to create an impact on the fabric. Select some areas in which to apply free running stitch as a filling stitch. A) Define these areas by first stitching an outline. B) Next, proceed to fill in the areas. C) Work very narrow zigzag and

satin stitches that are just slightly wider than the straight stitch. If these stitches are applied to excess, or are too wide, they may take over the whole piece, so use them with discretion. D) Cable stitch may be applied to create a thicker line that will quickly build up greater density.

THE PILLAR SAMPLER

This sampler, because of the weights and properties of the fabrics used, should be one of the easiest to embellish without using an embroidery frame. It combines layering and cut-back appliqué with automatic and free machine embroidery.

The fabrics have been selected to work together sympathetically. The bottom layer is either of silk or nylon organza. This allows the fabric to be maneuvered freely under the machine without the need for a frame, and helps to reduce the weight and rigidity of the entire piece. The middle layer of fabric may be wool felt, a synthetic felt, or a fairly stiff wool fabric such as Melton cloth. This middle layer helps to provide sufficient rigidity and loft to

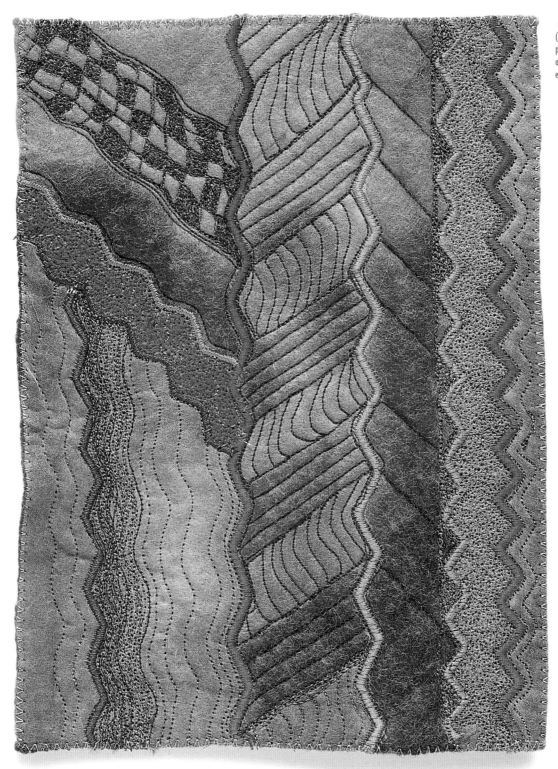

◄ 5-18 *Pillar Sampler* 13 x 18 cm (5 x 7″) A quilted effect was produced by working a combination of automatic and free machine embroidery techniques.

assist the embroiderer in working freely without a frame.

Free machine techniques are not always a success on wool-type fabrics since many stitches simply sink into the fabric, never to be seen again, or the stitching may distort the fabric.

By using silk organza as the top layer, however, one is able to cut back some areas of the top fabric, and still work stitches over the remaining organza without creating distortion. The layering helps to reduce distortion and the tendency for stitches to sink into wool is turned into an advantage, increasing the contrast between the wool and organza areas. The stitches worked over the organza will rest on the surface of the fabric while those that are worked on the middle layer will sink in, and the lustrous organza will contrast with the matte finish of the middle fabric.

Pieces embroidereded in this way are suitable for wall hangings, bags and book covers.

Stitch an outline around areas that are to receive filling stitches. This will control and stabilize the more heavily stitched areas and help to avoid distortion. Nine lines divide this sampler into ten separate shapes within the outer frame. The design lines may be transferred to the top layer of the fabric, using techniques as shown on page 45.

REQUIREMENTS

FABRICS

The bottom layer is of silk or nylon organza; the following, middle, layer is wool felt, wool Melton cloth, or a similar fabric, and the top layer is silk organza. Approximately 13 x 18 cm (5 x 7″) of each are needed.

THREADS

Use machine embroidery threads.

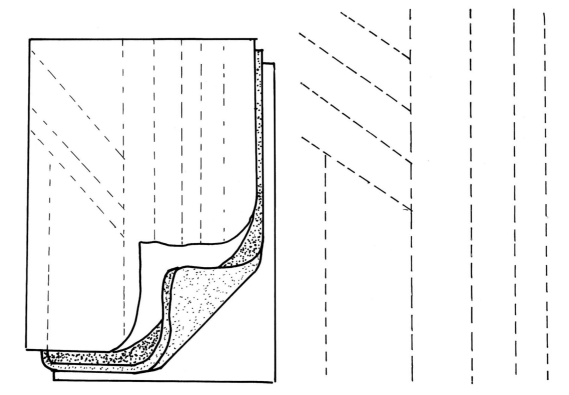

▶ 5-19 Step 1

▶▶ 5-20 Step 2

NEEDLE

Use a size 80 (12) needle – embroidery, quilting, topstitch or regular, as suits the threads and fabrics.

Step 1

Leaving a border around the edge of the piece, assemble the fabric layers and baste them together in the usual way. These layers form the structural base of the sampler.

Step 2

Select automatic stitching mode and apply satin stitch or some other simple decorative stitch along the marked dividing lines. Keep the design simple at this stage to allow for further embellishment. Use the same stitch for each line, but add a little extra flavour by varying the stitch width (a total of five stitch widths were used here) and by changing thread colour on each line. The stitch width should not be greater than 2.5 mm ($^1/_8$″). Use the satin stitch or embroidery presser foot.

Step 3

Cut back the organza on alternate areas, cutting close to the stitching lines. This will expose some areas of the middle fabric and leave other areas of organza intact.

Step 4

Attach the darning foot to the machine, lower the feed dogs and embroider the central area of the sampler first. Fill areas with free running stitch in very compact circular patterns. Try a different filling stitch on organza areas not yet stitched. Contrast densely packed stitching areas with more sparsely applied stitches in other areas.

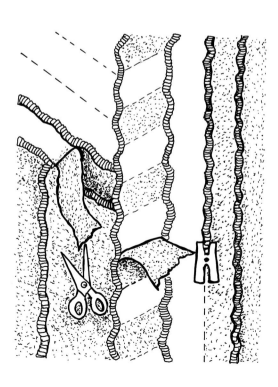

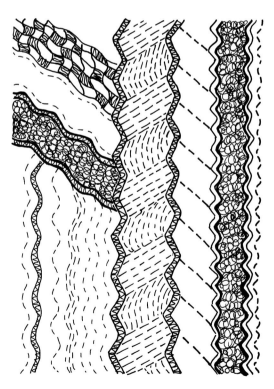

◀◀ 5-21 Step 3

◀ 5-22 Step 4

CHAPTER 6

~

SAMPLERS THAT GROW OUT OF GRIDS

▶ 6-2 *Woven Band Sampler*
18 x 20 cm (7 x 8") This piece was a colour study developed from a Gustav Klimt painting. Instead of paints I used fabrics, threads, ribbons, and cords to represent the emotion of the colours found in the painting.

◄◄ 6-1 *Genesis*
84 x 84 cm (33 x 33") - Patterned markings and veins were first richly and lavishly machine embroidered using free running stitch and free satin stitch on what first began life as a pair of two-arm length butterfly wings. The wings were nice, but I decided they needed a new life. The wings were cut into irregular patches and laid over a dark blue background fabric. Other pieces of fabric, chosen for colour mixing, were inserted under and over the patches. The patches and added fabric were tacked down on the background fabric and appliquéd. The whole piece was quilted all over using free running stitch and free satin stitch.

WOVEN BANDS SAMPLER

THIS SAMPLER, which measures about 18 x 20 cm (7 x 8"), acts as a quick colour study in fabrics, threads, and ribbons. There is no need to search painstakingly for exact colours, nor any need to plan out where each strip is woven in or where to stitch. Just find a pleasing picture and pick out materials with colours that are near matches. Weave these into your sampler. In the example, the object was to find complementary colours and use them in proportions that would make the yellows and gold more striking. The complementary colours were added towards the end of the process because they were the thinnest items used (machine and hand embroidery threads). Their addition to the colour balance was very gradual and did not quickly change the nature of the dominant colour. The complementary colours should not cover as much space on the sampler as does the dominant colour.

Be patient with this sampler and let it grow. Continue to push the artistic boundaries until the colours are powerful and zingy. The example contains seven different colours, including gold cotton, green khaki cotton, pink silk and yellow satin. Used in the collage are ribbons and strips of fabric, most of them in gold metallic and yellow colours. Complementary colours include royal blue, purples, oranges, greens, turquoise, gold, and pink. Many beginners are reluctant to push to the extreme when working with colours – push on! The initial fabrics will influence succeeding colour choices. Look for the subtle hints of colour peeking out here and there from between the cracks after the ribbons have been woven over the top.

PROJECT HINTS

Pin the work on a wall, and look at it from a distance every once in a while. This is a good way of checking to see how the piece is evolving. From the beginning, try to avoid the pitfall of having too many preconceived notions about the finished embroidery. Each step will alter the appearance of the work. Continue to view the piece periodically. Each time, try to view it with fresh eyes to re-evaluate what is needed to keep the embroidery evolving.

REQUIREMENTS

BACKGROUND FABRIC
Use calico, muslin, or heavier cotton, approximately 23 x 25 cm (9 x 10").

COLLAGE/APPLIQUÉ FABRICS
Choose shades and tones of colours within the colour range only. Fabrics should be of a similar weight and not have a surface finish that would be distracting. The example uses quilting cottons, satins and silks. Pieces are small – your scrap heap may produce some pieces about 10 cm (4") in length in the selected colour range. About 1/2 m (1/2 yd) of any of the following in widths of between 6 mm and 2 cm (1/4 and 3/4") could be used: metallic, sheer, or satin ribbon, sequin waste, lamé or net cut into strips, craft sequins on a thread, and twisted or round cords.

MACHINE EMBROIDERY THREADS
Choose a variety from the colour range of the background, but predominantly select colours in the complementary range.

HAND STITCHING THREAD
Use cotton floss or cotton perlé (pearl).

NEEDLE
Use a sharp needle for hand stitching; for machine work, use an embroidery, topstitch or regular size 80 (12) needle or as small as can be used.

Step 1
Baste fabrics of the chosen colour scheme to the background fabric. Overlap layers as seems pleasing to the eye. There is no need to butt fabrics against each

▶ 6-3 Step 1

▶▶ 6-4 Step 2

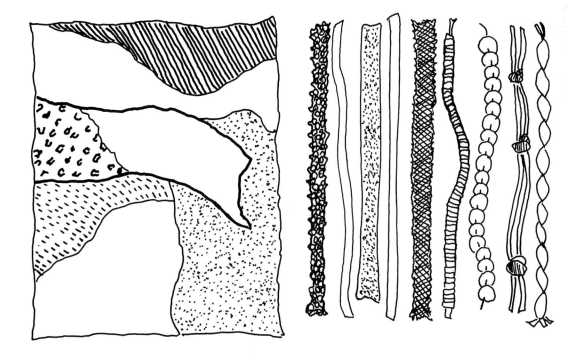

other. Use automatic straight or zigzag stitch to attach the fabric to the background.

Step 2
Prepare ribbons and cords by laying them on a sheet of white paper to isolate them from the background and other materials. Check that the selection contains contrasting widths and tones. Include ribbons and nets that are gauzy or sheer. Try knotting some threads or cords to create texture, and add some twisted cords.

Step 3
Lay ribbons, strips of net, fabrics, sequins and cords horizontally over the collage of background fabric. Lay on the brightest and shiniest colours first, including different widths and tones of the colour scheme. Move these around until they look balanced, but not necessarily symmetrical. Pin them to hold them in position.

Step 4
Weave some of the strips vertically through the horizontal threads. Let colours dictate the pattern; try to distribute different tones and colours throughout the

piece. Pin the strips to secure them in position. Continue weaving strips both vertically and horizontally through the piece until a satisfactory arrangement has been created. For the time being, do not add any complementary colours. This stage should still be restricted to tones of one colour.

Step 5
Complementary colours should now be worked into the sampler. Use long, free machine stitches at the junctions of ribbons and strips. Lay threads down both horizontally and vertically. Do not be surprised if some areas get totally covered with stitches. This will help to hold the whole structure together.

Step 6
Apply some running stitches by hand. Select some hand embroidery threads in complementary colours. Stranded cotton is handy, as you can select from one to six strands, allowing varying proportions of colour to be incorporated. If more colour is needed in any particular area, simply stitch in more cotton strands or an even heavier thread. Work in both directions.

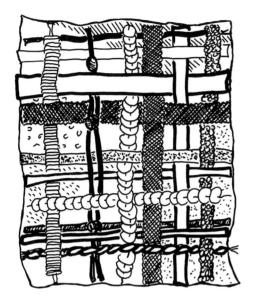

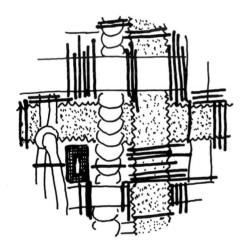

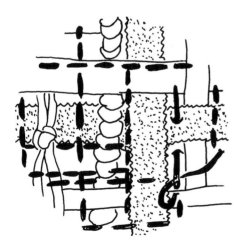

CONTINUOUS STITCH
STAR SAMPLER

◀ 6-5 Step 4

This quilted sampler, measuring 14 x 18 cm (5 1/2 x 7″), uses a basic grid as a guide to lay-ing down an organic or geometric figure. This particular method of quilting depends upon having a grid of automatic stitches (squares or rectangles) laid down over the fabric. This grid not only forms a part of the decorative element, but will be an aid to controlling the shape of the pattern that will follow. The crossing points of the grid will act as aiming points for the needle. The individual pattern inscribed within each area of the grid could be almost any shape.

◀ 6-6 Step 5

Note that two machine set-ups are used for this sampler. The machine is first set for automatic stitching to stitch the grid; you then change the settings to the free machine mode to embroider the filler patterns.

When the grid is complete, enter one area of it and apply free running stitch. The sampler is stitched in one continuous flow, so it is necessary to stitch along some lines twice in order to reach the succeeding square. Work out a sequence that will keep repitition to a minimum. If your chosen fabric is particularly stretchy, work in horizontal or vertical rows, not diagonally, as shown in the steps. Continue on through each area, enter-ing each at the same point. This will create a pattern that looks consistent over the whole piece. Make the areas of the grid only as large as is comfortable to fill with free run-ning stitch with precision. To begin with, try 2.5 cm (1″) grids.

◀ 6-7 Step 6

This technique will look vibrant and exciting if it is produced on mottled, coloured or hand-painted muslin or quilting fabric.

AVOIDING PROBLEMS

It is important to prevent the fabric from puckering while the grid is being stitched. The fabric may pucker either because the fabrics were not properly basted together, or because the automatic straight stitch length is too short. The stitches will need to be a bit longer than for ordinary sewing to accommodate the thickness of the fabric layers. Try using spray starch on the top and bottom fabrics to stiffen these a little before basting layers together. This will make the sandwiched layers easier to handle during stitching.

You might opt to use silk or nylon organza rather than cotton for top and bottom fabrics. These will glide a little more easily over the bed of the sewing machine.

Those who are not very practised in free running stitch without a frame can begin the stitching at an easy entry and exit point, such as the corner of grid. However, the free running pattern can enter a grid at any point, and rows may be worked side-by-side as well as on the diagonal.

REQUIREMENTS

FABRICS
Use a cotton fabric or silk organza for the top and bottom and a thin batting for the middle layer.

THREADS
For the grid, use machine embroidery or dressmakers' thread in a colour that will match or blend into the background fabric. Use a range of machine embroidery threads for the stars.

NEEDLE
Use a size 80 (12) quilting or embroidery needle. If the thread does not readily pass throught the needle, change to a size 90 (14).

Step 1
Baste together three layers of fabric. You may use either a cotton or a silk organza for both the top and bottom fabrics. Plan the basting so that grid lines will not lie directly over the top of the basting lines.

Step 2
Use automatic straight stitch 3 to 3.5 mm ($^1/_8$ to $^3/_{16}$″ length) to stitch the grid, stitching through the layers. Work from the centre outwards, making first a vertical line and then a horizontal line, and continuing out to the edges of the fabric. Remove basting threads as work progresses. The preparation of the fabric and stitching of the grid are the most critical steps of the procedure. Try to prevent any puckering of the material (see Avoiding Problems).

Step 3
Using free running stitch without a frame, begin stitching a pattern somewhere near the centre of the piece. Avoid starting at one of the outside edges. The example has a star shape within each grid area. To reproduce this pattern, manipulate the fabric under the needle to follow the arrows from A to H. Enter the second square with the needle at the top left corner.

◀ 6-8 *Continuous Stitch Star Sampler* 13 x 18 cm (5 x 7″) A series of patterns are stitched within the grid structure using machine embroidery threads on quilter's weight cotton fabric.

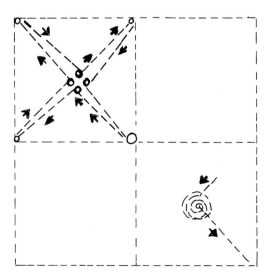

◀ 6-9 Step 3

▶ 6-10 Step 4

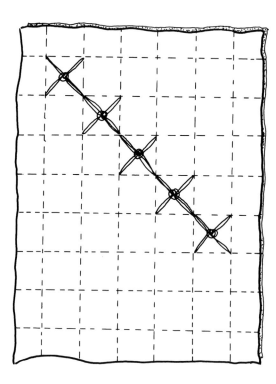

Step 4

On the example, the pattern has been worked diagonally from square to square. The pattern stitching proceeds through the squares from corner to corner, stopping in the centre, then out to the next corner. The second and succeeding squares could be stitched over a slightly different route. It is immaterial whether one part of the star has more than one or two lines of stitching. Find a good entry and exit point that will be consistent with continuous working of the squares.

Step 5

Continue to build outwards from the centre of the piece in alternating rows. You will find that it can take a little time to develop an even stitch length.

Step 6

Try to create some additional patterns to use with the continuous stitch technique. Using a piece of graph paper, draw some continuous line patterns without lifting the pencil. Any one of these might evolve into an attractive pattern to use for this technique.

▶ 6-11 Step 5

▶▶ 6-12 Step 6

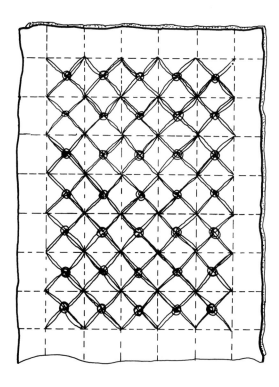

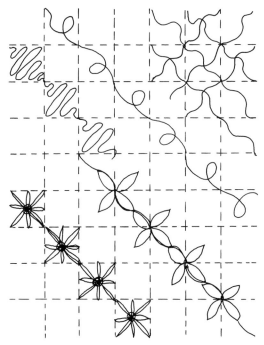

SUN MOTIF SAMPLER

This sampler is an extension of the stitch and design idea from the star sampler, and is intended to advance the skills introduced in the latter. In this instance, the background fabric is first divided into grids of two different sizes. A simple sun motif is added to the smaller grid areas, while larger, more elaborate, sun motifs are worked into the larger areas. Some of the squares are cut away to reveal more colour interest. Satin and zigzag stitches are used to outline all the squares.

TIPS AND HINTS

Note that the sampler begins with an automatic stitch set-up, moves into the free machine embroidery mode, and then returns to the automatic set-up. For a successful piece, follow the steps below in the order given. The last step of this project is to stitch over the grid lines.

For simplicity, this sampler may be worked with as few as two colours. However, many colour combinations may be used to create highlights and add bits of colour interest. It is conceivable that as many as 10 colours could be worked into the design. One line of satin stitch might use as many as six changes of thread colour. Needless to say, this involves much threading and re-threading of the top machine thread, but a little patience will pay off in a stunning combination of colours. Leave long thread ends on the surface until they get in the way. Finally, take all loose threads to the back with a hand sewing needle, and tie them off. When you combine many different techniques on a small piece, it is all but impossible to have a neat reversible backing. The solution is to slipstitch a lining fabric over the back.

REQUIREMENTS

FABRICS

You will need two top fabrics of silk or quilting cotton (each approximately 30 × 30 cm/12 × 12 in); they should be of a similar weight and of a type that will not easily fray. These are backed by thin batting and, if necessary for ease of stitching, a backing fabric of organza or organdie, to make four layers in total.

THREADS

Use machine embroidery threads.

NEEDLE

Select either a size 80 (12) needle or one appropriate to the threads being used.

Step 1

Transfer or mark grid lines on either the top or background fabric. Baste the fabric layers together, taking care to leave excess fabric (borders) around the edges on all sides. Read all information contained in the instructions for the star sampler for hints and tips on working grids and patterns on the fabric.

Step 2

Use automatic straight stitch to stitch the grid lines on the basted fabrics; perhaps, as here, the grid might echo an existing pattern. Set the stitch length to between 2.5 and 3 mm ($^1/_{16}$ and $^1/_8$″). Use as small a needle as will accommodate the thread being used. Match the thread colour to that of the fabric. Randomly cut back squares of top fabric, using small sharp scissors.

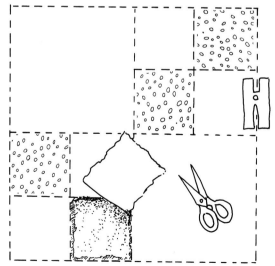

◄ 6-14 Step 2

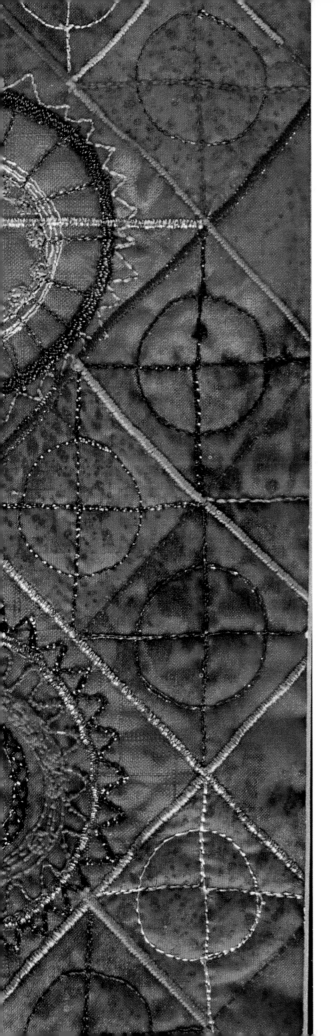

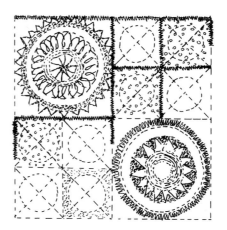

◀ 6-15 *Step 5*

Step 3

Proceed to stitch motifs in the large squares, using free machine embroidery. Use any small circular template at hand (such as a small tumbler) to trace a round shape on the fabric. Place the fabric in a frame to help stabilize the large patterned areas during machining. Outline each large circle, using free running stitch in any type of patterning that seems suitable. Avoid overworking the circles, or a manipulated fabric (see following sampler) will appear.

Step 4

Remove the frame and apply continuous line stitching in the smaller grid areas. Work the smaller circles and lines from square-to-square as with the star sampler. As you stitch each small grid area, plan ahead to fix entry and exit points that will avoid the larger areas that are already stitched. To avoid stop-and-start stitch sequences, let the needle stitch along already-sewn grid lines to travel from one point to another.

Step 5

Using a satin stitch/embroidery foot on the machine, embroider over the grid lines with automatic zigzag and satin stitch. Use machine embroidery threads and change the top thread frequently to create colour interest throughout the piece. The stitch width may remain constant (2 mm/$^1/_8$″ maximum); alternatively, you may choose to vary the width, but try not to detract from the patterns within the grids. Work the zigzag or satin stitch in continuous lines.

◀◀ 6-13 *Sun Motif Sampler*
20 x 20 cm (8 x 8″) This piece begins with a complex network of two different sized stacked grids. Two different sized circular sun patterns were worked in a variety of thread colours over the hand painted fabric.

▶▶ *6-16 Manipulated Fabric Sampler 21 x 21 cm (8 x 8") The base fabric for this sampler began with strips of fabric fused to a piece of iron-on interfacing. A grid was worked over the fabric and then a series of circles were created in each square using free running stitch.*

MANIPULATED FABRIC SAMPLER

One of the differences between creating a design with needle and fabric as opposed to pencil and paper is that the fabric may be manipulated and moulded as if it were a living thing. This characteristic of fabric can change the very nature of a design. It is quite enlightening to explore this capability, which can add another dimension to one's work.

An initial concept will often suggest a further development. A series of samplers will provide beneficial reference points to inspire any number of possible creations.

Most of the time we work to keep fabric smooth and even, striving to avoid puckers. On some occasions, however, the intentional buckling, pulling and furrowing of a fabric can provide a character and beauty produced in no other way. Different fabrics will produce different effects when they are pushed to the limits. For this example, which measures 20 cm (8") square, a grid was laid down and a circle inscribed in each square. This action produced a regular and repeating distortion of the fabric. It is best to work this technique without a frame, but if a frame is used, make sure the fabric is loosely mounted. As with previous examples, the machine is first set up for automatic stitching to sew the grid lines; you then switch to free machine mode, using free running stitch to produce the manipulation inside the grids.

FINISHING THE SAMPLER

Avoid working the free running stitch circles up to the edges of the fabric. This will not produce the same effect. Leave an unstitched fabric border of about 5 cm (2") on all sides to be used as fabric handholds while free machining. Finish off the edges with automatic straight stitch, and trim away any excess fabric.

REQUIREMENTS

FABRICS

The top fabric is a piece of cotton, silk or other light-weight, yielding fabric, 30 cm (12") square. This is backed by thin batting. A thin backing fabric may also be added (see Step 1, below).

THREADS

Machine embroidery threads in various colours are used throughout.

NEEDLE

Use a size 80 (12) or 90 (14) embroidery or quilting needle.

Step 1

Mark the grid on the top or bottom layer of the fabric. Baste together the top fabric and thin batting. If the latter is fairly firm, no bottom fabric is required. If not, include a thin bottom fabric with the basted fabric layers. The basted layers of fabric must be easy to push and pull around over the bed of the machine.

Step 2

Using automatic straight stitch, lay down a basic grid. Follow directions given in the star sampler. Here, the

▶▶ *6-17 Step 1*

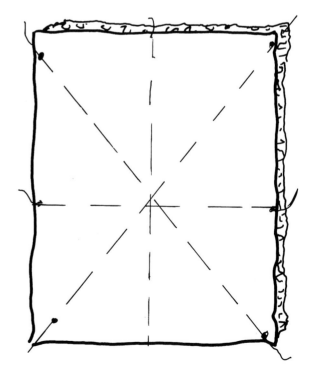

▶ 6-18 Step 2

▶▶ 6-19 Step 3

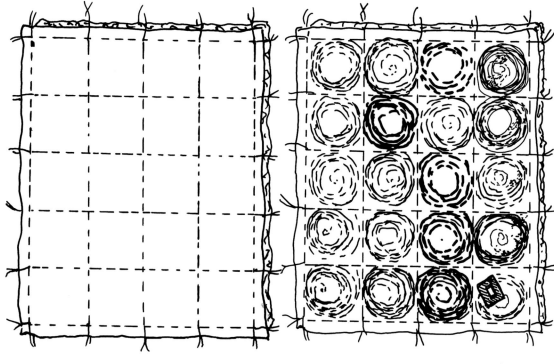

▶ 6-20 Step 4

▶▶ 6-21 Step 5

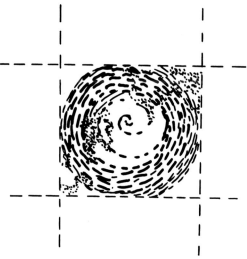

grid is formed of 2.5 cm (1″) squares, but any shape of grid could be used for this type of sampler.

Step 3

Set the machine for free running stitch and position the centre of the fabric under the needle. Begin sewing a circle within one of the squares, making as many as 15 circles around the perimeter. Stitch until a

raised bubble of fabric appears. Unless you intend the bubble to be flattened, avoid stitching in the centre of the circle.

Step 4

Continue to make free running stitch circles until all the squares are filled. Use any colour of thread for each circle, but change colours from time to time to create an ever-changing play of light.

Step 5

Use the fabric in the creation of a further developed item. The example has been formed into a roll. Now, what could the bubbles possibly be? They protrude 5 mm to 1 cm (¹/4 to ³/8″) above the surface of the fabric. Are they barnacles on a rock, mushrooms on a tree, or something else?

◄ 6-22 *Sorting Out the Shell Collection* 30 x 46 cm (12 x 18″) - Many different sizes and shapes of shells were scanned into the sewing machine memory and stitched on cotton and felt background fabrics. Random Strip Patchwork was placed on a background fabric and stitched down. Sizes and shapes were chosen at random. *Penny Butterworth*

▶ 6-23 Photo - Kenji Nagai
Sinagua Tribute - On a trip to Arizona, I saw aboriginal cliff dwellings for the first time. I was moved by their ingenuity and beauty. This piece is a tribute to the Sinagua Tribe, farming peoples, who built their incredible homes, then abandoned them, and moved on for reasons that are not known. The border squares are designs from pottery shards found in these dwellings, often undisturbed for centuries.

Jane Kenyon

CHAPTER 7

FINISHING TOUCHES

▶ 7-3 Step 1

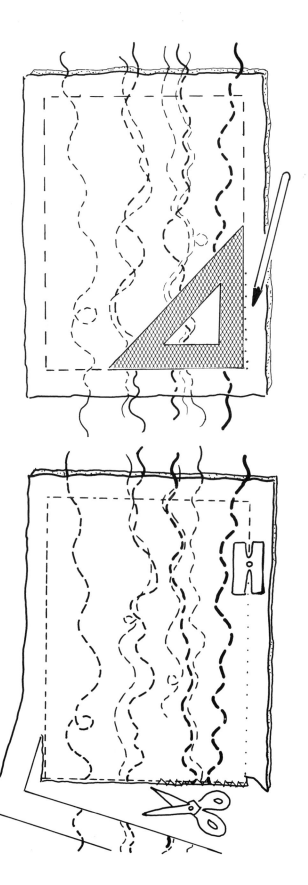

COMING TO THE END of an embroidered project can be an anticlimax. What to do now? The format in which almost any graphic work of art is presented may either enhance and complete it or visually diminish and dissipate its impact. Must it be matted or framed? No embroidery seems finished until some kind of complementary edge or border has been applied. Badly designed edges, however, detract from the work they surround. It is therefore vital to find the finish that will enhance the work. Try creating a few samples to retain as your basic edge vocabulary. Size, shape, and colour are factors that must complement the work at hand. The following pages contain some edge techniques and samples that may offer an inspiration for your own work, including some that are particularly suited to samplers. The examples are but the tip of the iceberg, so look in other needlework books and magazines. Be sure to allow sufficient time to give this all-important finish to a sampler.

▶ 7-4 Step 2

FINISHING A SAMPLER

One of the advantages of the following method is that it secures the edges of the work. This finishing method is best facilitated if the directions on preparing a sampler (see pages 40 and 41) are followed.

Step 1
Using a right angle and pencil, mark off the perimeter of the work to its finished size. Keep the corners square, and opposite sides the same length.

Step 2
Using programmed straight stitch, stitch along the marked lines, going twice around the perimeter. Carefully cut around the outside of the rows of stitching to remove excess fabric.

◀◀ 7-1 *Nasturtium Pillow*
25 cm (10˝) diameter The subject came directly from nature. The artist did colour studies and experimented with edge treatments to find the best solution to portray her concept. Narrow width zigzag stitch was worked around flower and leaf edges. Satin stitch cording, some with wire core, were used to represent vines and tendrils. *Cathy Marston*

◄ 7-2 *Nasturtium Pillow* - Close up.

Step 3

The sample could be left at this stage, or a narrow zigzag stitch could be sewn over the edges. Use a thread that is as near to the edge colour as possible, or use nylon (invisible) thread. Avoid using satin stitch over the edges – it has a way of dominating the whole work.

DISPLAYING SAMPLES

When the sample is completed, it may be mounted on a card. Apply a few inconspicuous hand stitches through the fabric and matt card to secure it. Use very small stitches on the front and long stitches at the back. Choose as large a needle as you require to do the job and use a thread that blends into the fabric. Double-sided tape could also be used to fasten the sample to the card.

Another method is to mount the sample as one would a picture, behind a pre-cut window in a matt card. The sample may be lightly stretched and secured with tape to the back of the card. Make sure the work is positioned correctly within the window.

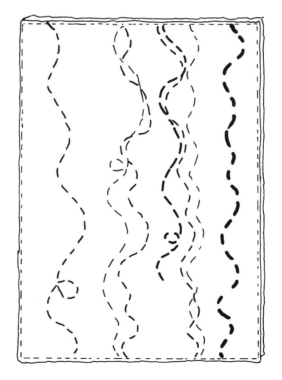

◄ 7-5 Step 3

▶ 7-6 Step 1

MOUNTING AND LACING AN EMBROIDERY

When it is desirable to have a rigid mounting for embroidery, it is necessary to attach it in some way to a very stiff card or board. The traditional and proven method is to lace the work across the back of the board. A work so mounted could be set in a frame, or combined with another matt board for display purposes.

For best effects, the embroidered piece should be limited to minimal finishing along the edges. If fraying is a problem, work a wide zigzag along the edges. Do not trim away the outer margins, as described for the previous method, and do not turn these edges under. Any of these finishing styles could add too much bulk for mounting and lacing.

Smaller samples may be mounted in this fashion, as may wall hangings, and book or box covers. The larger the piece to be mounted, the more rigid the mounting board/frame will need to be. If the mounting medium is not sufficiently stiff it may warp under lacing tensions. Cover the back of the mounted work with a fabric lining, slipstitching it in place along the edges.

▶ 7-7 Step 2

Step 1
Find or cut a mounting board (matt board) to a size that will allow an 8 cm (3″) margin around all sides of the work. Cut a piece of thin, soft batting to the exact size of the mounting board (or use iron-on batting). Apply this directly to the mounting board.

Step 2
Place the embroidered fabric on a table, right side down. Lay the mounting board, batting side down, over the work. The back sides of both the work and the mounting board will now be facing upwards.

Step 3
Wrap opposite edges of the embroidered work over the back of the mounting board. It can be handy to

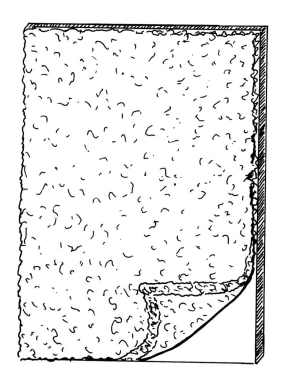

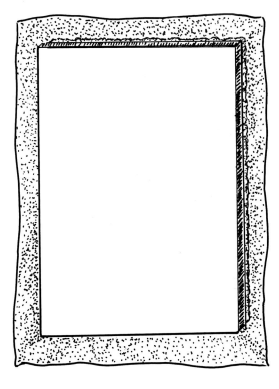

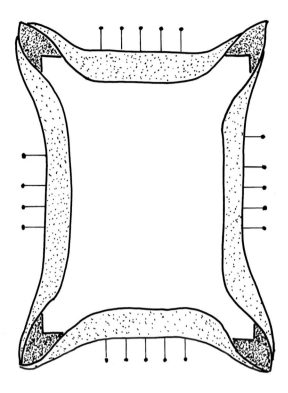

have some pins, such as craft-type clothes pins, to hold the fabric evenly and snugly in place while you prepare to do the lacing. Use many at close intervals.

◀ 7-8 Step 3

Step 4

Use a No. 12 pearlé (pearl cotton) or linen thread, and a sharp needle. Begin at the centre of one side and stitch across to the opposite side. Take the stitches over and under the fabric and try to angle the needle in the direction of the stitch. Secure the thread with a few back stitches.

Step 5

After stitching the first half, go back to the central starting point and stitch out to the other end until the two edges are completely laced. Try to apply consistent tension on the stitches in order to avoid stress points along the work. Too much tension might warp the mounting board.

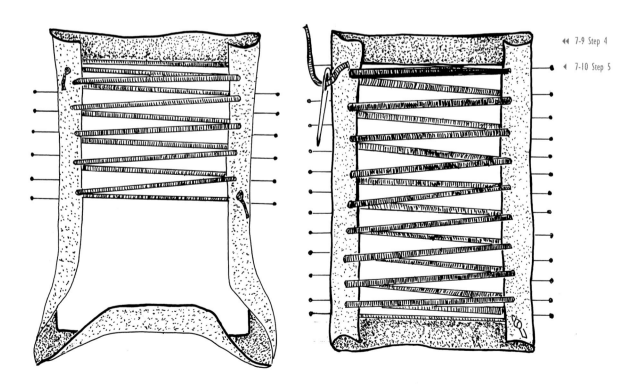

◀◀ 7-9 Step 4

◀ 7-10 Step 5

▶ 7-14 *The Plaice Mat - Decorative Cloth* - Close up.

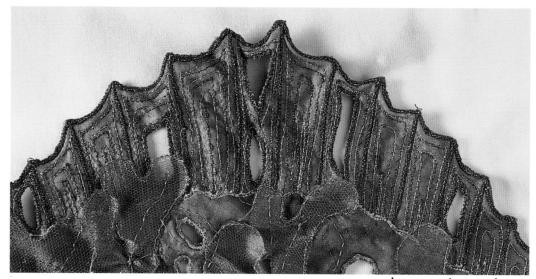

▶ 7-11 Step 6

▶▶ 7-12 Step 7

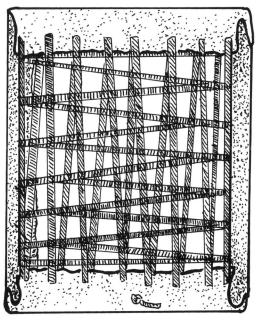

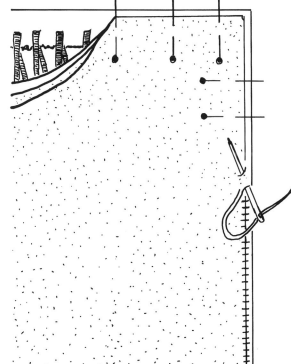

Step 6

Wrap the unlaced ends of the work over the back of the mounting board. Pin and hold in place as before. Begin lacing from the centre and continue as for the previous sides. Occasionally, weave the crossing threads through the previously applied ones. You may need to remove some fabric at corners to get them to lie flat. It is good practice to lace up to the corner before removing excess fabric. A few slip stitches in the corners can also help to keep them neat and secure.

Step 7

Place a lining fabric over the back of the laced work and turn the edges under. Pin this in place, leaving a small margin along the edges. Using a quilter's needle, slipstitch the lining fabric to the back of the work. Use dressmakers' thread or thread of equivalent strength.

▲ 7-13 *The Plaice Mat - Decorative Cloth*
25 x 30 cm (10 x 12") Edges were incorporated as
a special feature for the fish depicted in this work.
Much experimentation proved out a technique that
allowed the artist to stiffen the edges by stitching
over wire using zigzag and satin stitch. The fish
features stitched holes and the application of fabrics
using free machine embroidery. Nylon organza is the
main fabric used in this piece.   *Tessa Miller*

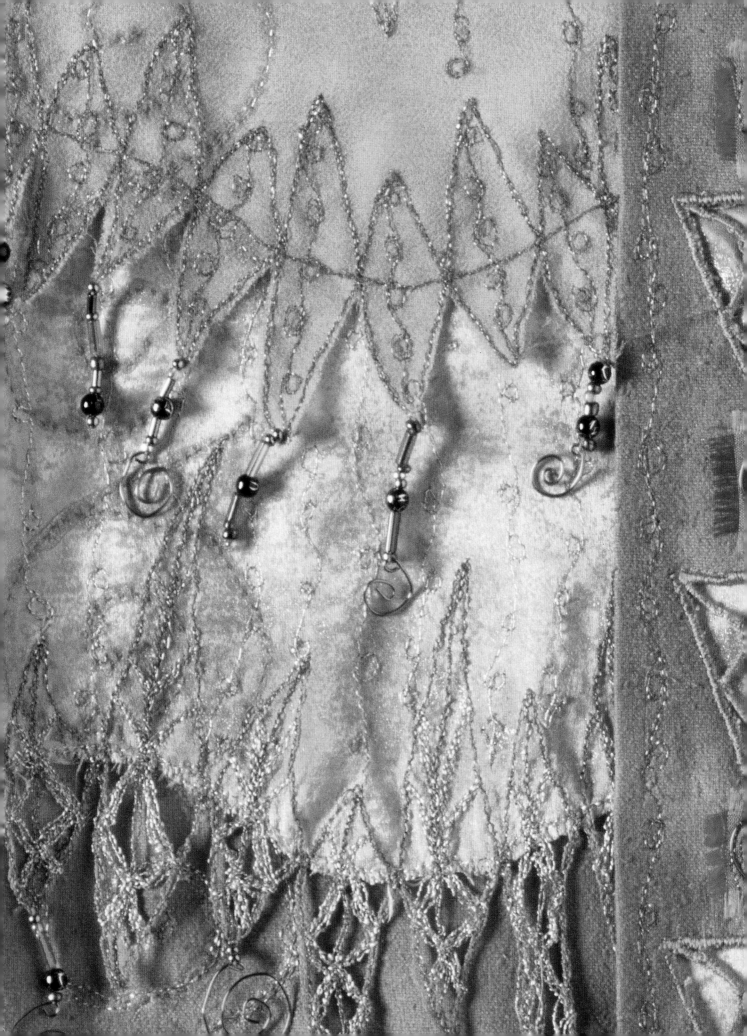

GALLERY

▲ G-I *Homage to Klee* 190 x 150 cm (76 x 60″) The artist, inspired by the paintings of Paul Klee, tried to represent his technique through the use of layered fabrics and free machine embroidery. Sheer fabrics were layered over more opaque ones to produce depth. Frayed muslin and scrim were applied to the collage to suggest texture and movement. Pulled threads allowed other colours to peep through. Brush marks were represented by free machining of long ovals with careful consideration of colours used.

Linda Kemshall

▶ G-2 Photo - Kenji Nagai. *Hopeful Giants* 95 x 110 cm (38 x 44″) This free machined wall hanging was inspired through the artist's residence in the coastal rain forest of British Columbia, and continually exposed to the debate between logging companies and environmentalists. She finds it shocking to be confronted by giant old growth forests standing adjacent to clear cut swaths. The artist wishes that this work will convey the hope that the powerfully beautiful ancient woodlands will be preserved.

Jane Kenyon

▲ G-3 *All the World's a Stage* 180 x 180 cm (7´6˝ x 6´6˝) The artist, often inspired by the works of Shakespeare, uses her very unique technique to graphically depict the tale in the form of a quilt. She first draws scenes from the story and assembles them in a sequence that highlights important parts of the story. Selected fabrics are then layered and placed in positions to be cut away revealing colours, textures and patterns. Outlines are first stitched from the back and then turned over for the cutting away and application of free satin stitch around figures and shapes to complete each scene. *Linda Straw*

◀ G-4 *All the World's a Stage* - Close up.

◀◀ G-5 *All the World's a Stage* - Close up.

◀ G-6 *A Minuscule Interior* - This work is a collection of miniaturised commonplace items. To give an idea of scale, the chair is 71 cm (28″) high. The embroidery was executed by using zigzag and satin stitch, combined with quilting techniques.

Penny Butterworth

◀◀ G-8 *Dollar Rug* - Pinking shears were used to cut circles of cotton and felt fabric. These were then folded in half and stitched down using straight stitch. Many rows of the overlapping half circles were stitched to a background fabric.

Penny Butterworth

▼ G-7 Close up of the chair back embroidery.

▶ G-9 Photo - Kenji Nagai
Seven Veils for the Goddess
53 x 135 cm (21 x 54˝) The seven
veils are pieced together by machine.
The central female figures are cut out
and filled with free machine lace.
Each figure is slightly different in
pose and character and represent
some of the wonderful qualities and
discoveries ascribed to early goddess-
es. They are suspended in a circle to
show unity, continuity, and the circle
of life.   *Jane Kenyon*

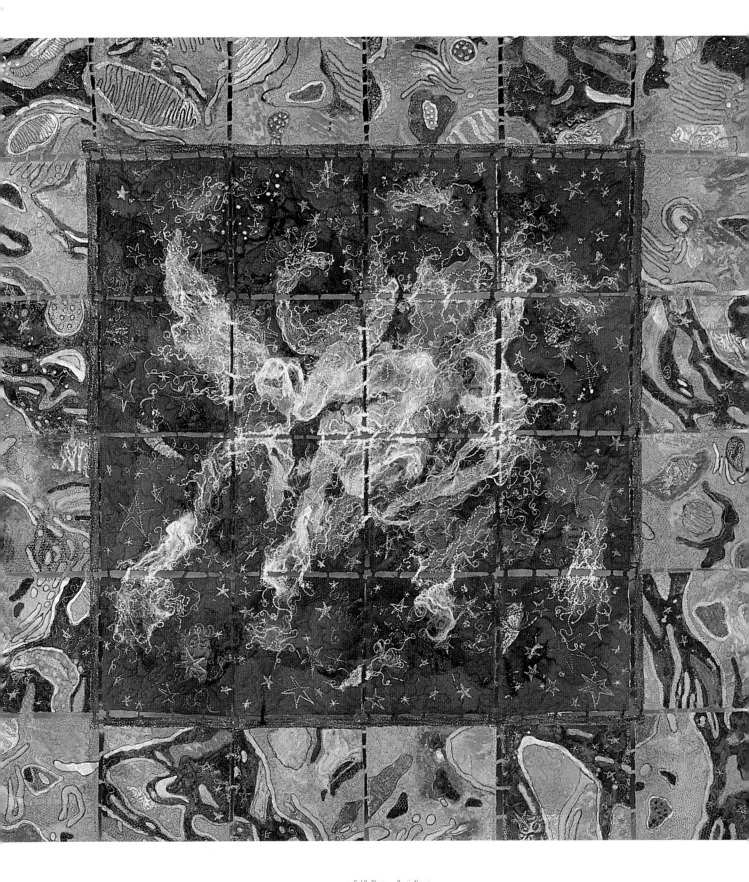

▲ G-10 Photo - Kenji Nagai

Journey Through Microspace 95 x 110 cm (38 x 44″) The central motif for this wall hanging was begun after watching the passage of the Hale-Bop comet. It represents the night sky, the universe, and space. The border is based upon electron micrographs of human cells. The juxtaposition of the two is a contrast in magnitude, focus, and perspective.   *Jane Kenyon*

▲ G-11 Photo - Mike Brown

Things Can Always Get Better - This waistcoat (vest) was the artist's therapeutic answer to working out breast cancer. The garment tells a story through its many embroidered panels. The left front shows a bird holding a man by a chain around his neck. Right front is a man furious because the fish are flying from his basket. Top of the back shows a man furious at a bird eating his crop, and bottom is a woman too busy to look at the fish the man has brought to her. Things could get better. Several different yarns and threads are machine stitched to the silk background to simulate the scales of a fish. Several decorative stitches and free machine embroidery was applied over the whole garment. *Virginia Schlosser*

▲ G-12 Photo - Mike Brown
Things Can Always Get Better - Back.

▶▶G-13 *Face Cloth* 25 x 38 cm (10 x 15″) Machine embroidery on silk organza. *Tricia Bunce*

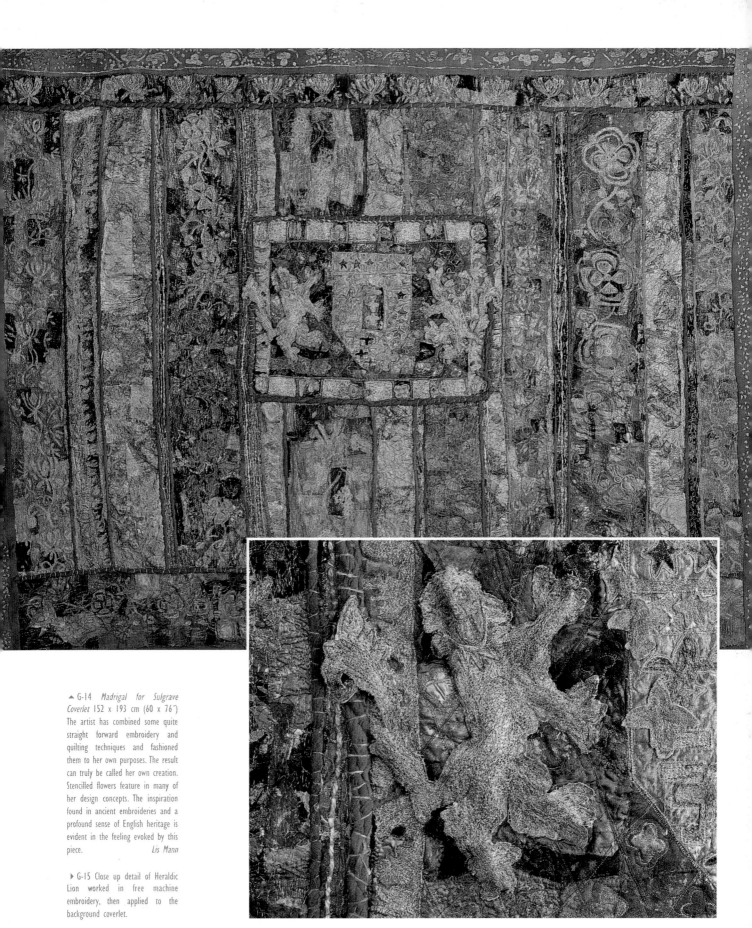

▲ G-14 *Madrigal for Sulgrave Coverlet* 152 x 193 cm (60 x 76″) The artist has combined some quite straight forward embroidery and quilting techniques and fashioned them to her own purposes. The result can truly be called her own creation. Stencilled flowers feature in many of her design concepts. The inspiration found in ancient embroideries and a profound sense of English heritage is evident in the feeling evoked by this piece. *Lis Mann*

▸ G-15 Close up detail of Heraldic Lion worked in free machine embroidery, then applied to the background coverlet.

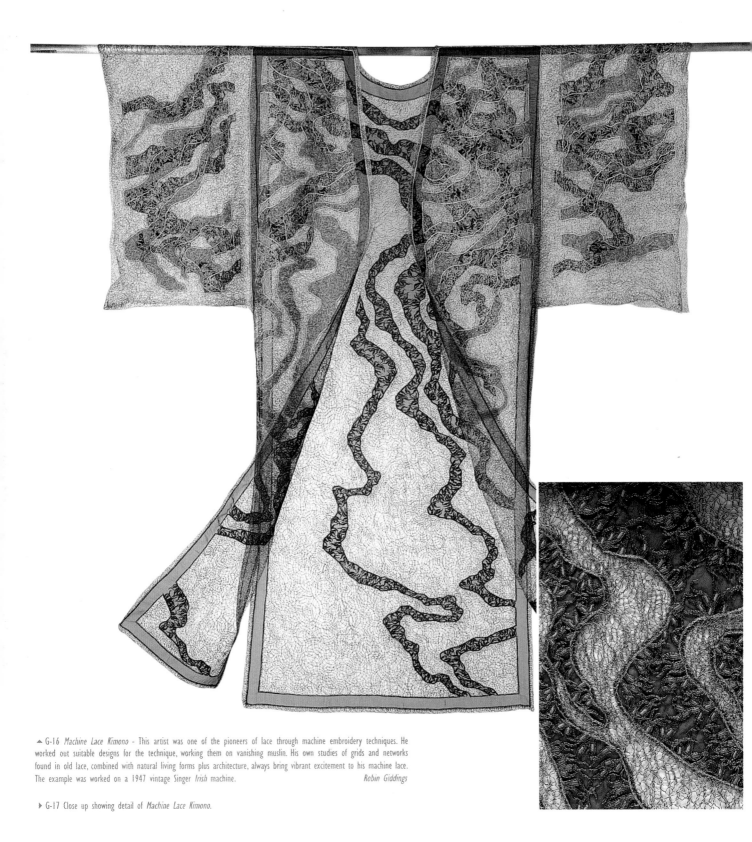

▲ G-16 *Machine Lace Kimono* - This artist was one of the pioneers of lace through machine embroidery techniques. He worked out suitable designs for the technique, working them on vanishing muslin. His own studies of grids and networks found in old lace, combined with natural living forms plus architecture, always bring vibrant excitement to his machine lace. The example was worked on a 1947 vintage Singer *Irish* machine.

Robin Giddings

▶ G-17 Close up showing detail of *Machine Lace Kimono*.

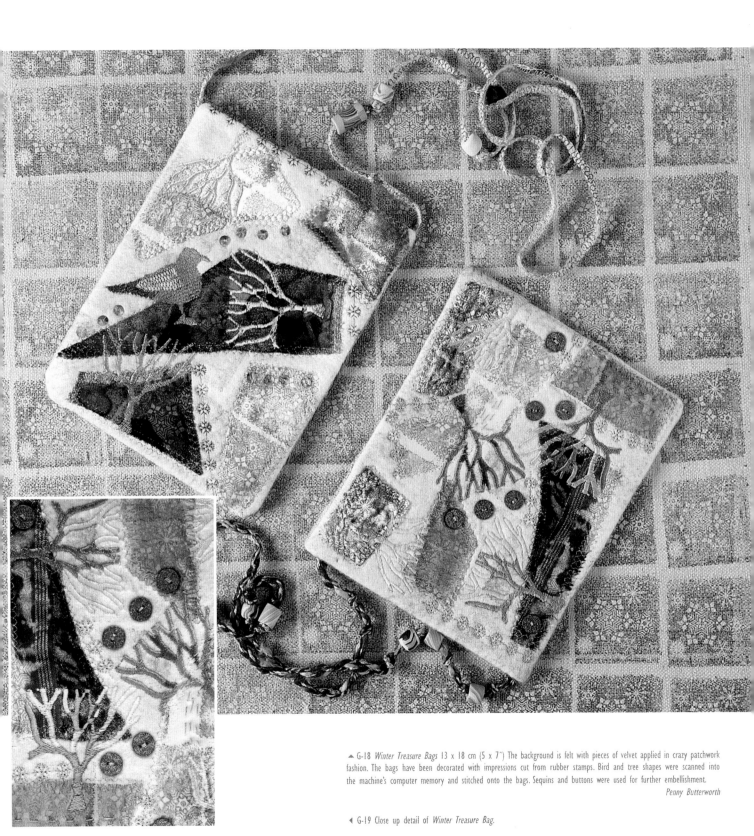

▲ G-18 *Winter Treasure Bags* 13 x 18 cm (5 x 7″) The background is felt with pieces of velvet applied in crazy patchwork fashion. The bags have been decorated with impressions cut from rubber stamps. Bird and tree shapes were scanned into the machine's computer memory and stitched onto the bags. Sequins and buttons were used for further embellishment.

Penny Butterworth

◀ G-19 Close up detail of *Winter Treasure Bag.*

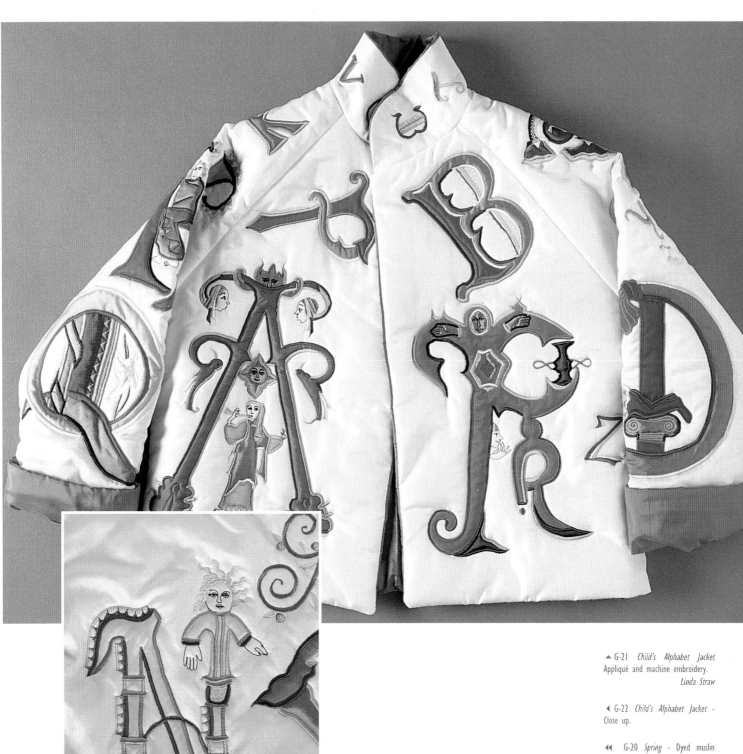

▲ G-21 *Child's Alphabet Jacket*
Appliqué and machine embroidery.
Linda Straw

◀ G-22 *Child's Alphabet Jacket* -
Close up.

◀◀ G-20 *Spring* - Dyed muslin
fabrics are pleated, tucked, and
applied to a background fabric. Trees
in the background are worked with
machine embroidery before being cut
out. Trees in the foreground are
worked on dissolving fabric. The
foreground is worked with pleats,
twin needle tucks, free machine
embroidery and hand stitching on
dyed fabric painted with acrylics.
Julia Barton

BIBLIOGRAPHY

Benson, Dorothy   **Machine Embroidery,**
Singer Sewing Machine Co. Ltd., London, 1946
Your Machine Embroidery,
Sylvan Press Ltd, London, 1952

Early Decorative Textiles,
The Hamlyn publishing Group, London, 1966

Gudjonson, Elsa E.   **'Traditional Icelandic Embroidery',**
Iceland Review, Reykjavik, 1982

Harding, Val Campbell   **Fabric Painting for Embroidery,**
B. T. Batsford Ltd., London, 1996

Harker, Gail   **Machine Embroidery,**
Merehurst, London, 1990

Naylor, Marie   **Authentic Indian Design,**
Dover Books, New York, 1975

Parker, Julie   **All About Cotton,**
Rain City Publishing, Seattle, 1993

SUPPLIERS

The following companies are distributors or suppliers of the products listed:

USA

Jacquard Fabric Paints:
Rupert, Gibbon, and Spider Inc.
P.O. Box 425
Healdsburg, California 95449
Toll Free from US: 1 800 442 0445
International Tel.: (+1) 707 433 9577
www.jacquardproducts.com

Kreinik metallic braids:
Kreinik Threads
3106 Lord Baltimore Dr.
Suite 101
Baltimore, Maryland 21244
Consumer Hotline (from US): 1 800
537 2166
International Tel.: (+1) 410 281 0040
E-mail: kreinik@kreinik.com
www.kreinik.com

Madeira machine embroidery
threads:
Madeira USA
30 Bayside Court
P.O. Box 6068
Laconia, New Hampshire 03246
Toll Free from US: 800 225 3001
International Tel.: (+1) 603 528 2944
Fax: 603 528 4264

Supply of sewing machines:
Pfaff Sewing Machines
P.O. Box 458012
3100 Viking Park Way
Westlake, Ohio 44145
Tel.: 440 808 6550
Fax: 440 847 0001
www.pfaff.com

Timtex interfacing:
Timber Lane Press
24350 N. Rimrock Rd.
Hayden, Idaho 83835
Tel./Fax: 208 765 3353
E-mail: qltblox@earthlink.net

Gail Harker's Books:
Gail Harker Creative Studies Center
1751 NE Goldie Street, Bldg. B
Oak Harbor, Washington 98253
Tel.: 360 279 2105
Fax: 360 279 0420
E-mail: gailembr@gte.net
www.gailcreativestudies.com

UNITED KINGDOM

Kreinik metallic braids and ribbons:
Coats Crafts UK
McMullen Rd.
Darlington, Co. Durham DL1 1YQ
Tel.: 01325 394394
Fax: 01325 394200

Non-woven interfacings, stabilizers:
Freudeuberg Non-wovens Ltd
The Vilene Corporation
Lowfield Business Park
Elland, West Yorkshire HX5 9DX
Tel.: 01422 327900

Nylon organza fabric:
Borovik Fabric Ltd.
16 Berwick Street
London W1F 0HP
Tel.: 020 7437 2180

Ribbons, threads, fabric:
John Lewis
278-306 Oxford Street
London W1A 1EX
Tel.: 020 7629 7711
(and branches nationwide)

Supply of Sewing Machines:
Viking Sewing Machines (UK) Ltd.
Viking House
Cheddar Business Park
Wedmore Road
Cheddar, Somerset BS27 3EB
Tel.: 01934 744533
Fax: 01934 744811
E-mail: uk.info@pfaff.com
www.pfaff.com

Wide variety of needlework supplies:
Mace & Nairn
P.O. Box 5626
Northampton
NN7 2BF
Tel.: 01604 864869
Fax.: 01604 864924
www.mace-and-nairn.freeserve.co.uk

Madeira machine embroidery
threads:
Maderia Threads (UK) Ltd.
Thirsk Industrial Park
York Road
Thirsk, New Yorkshire Y07 3BX
Tel.: 01845 524880
Fax: 01845 525046
Email: info@madeira.co.uk
www.madeira.co.uk

NEW ZEALAND

Kreink metallic braids and ribbons:
Craftco Ltd.
8 Moncur Place
P.O. Box 8086
Christchurch, 8034

INDEX